The Book of BOSTON

THE FEDERAL PERIOD
1775 to 1837

By MARJORIE DRAKE ROSS

With photographs by Samuel Chamberlain

HASTINGS HOUSE PUBLISHERS
New York

To

MY HUSBAND

John Clifford Ross

AND MY SON

John Drake Ross

This Book is
Affectionately Inscribed

Published simultaneously in Canada
by S. J. Reginald Saunders, Publishers, Toronto 2B.

Library of Congress Catalog Card Number: 61-14214

Printed in the United States of America

CONTENTS

ACKNOWLEDGMENTS

The following sources have been drawn upon in the compiling of this book. The author is very grateful for them.

Barber, John Warner, *Historical Collections – Every Town in Massachusetts*. Worcester: Dobbs, Howland and Company, 1839

Bulfinch, Ellen Susan, *The Life and Letters of Charles Bulfinch, Architect*. Boston: Houghton Mifflin Company, 1896

Chamberlain, Allen, *Beacon Hill Its Ancient Pastures and Early Mansions*. Boston: Houghton Mifflin Company, 1925

Colburn, James Smith, *Personal Memoirs*, 1780–1859

Comer, William R., *Landmarks in the Old Bay State*. Norwood: Norwood Press, 1911

Crawford, Mary Caroline, *Old Boston Days and Ways*. Boston: Little, Brown and Company, 1907

Crawford, Mary Caroline, *Romantic Days in the Early Republic*. Boston: Little, Brown and Company, 1912

Curtis, Caroline Gardiner, *Memories of Fifty Years in the Last Century*. Boston: Privately printed, 1947

Drake, Samuel Adams, *Old Landmarks and Historic Personages of Boston*. Boston: James R. Osgood, 1875

Ellis, George E., *History of the First Church of Boston*. Boston: *Hall and Whiting*, 1881

Hamlin, Talbot, *Greek Revival Architecture in America*. London, New York, Toronto: Oxford University Press, 1944

Higginson, Thomas Wentworth, *Life and Times of Stephen Higginson*. Boston: Houghton Mifflin and Company, 1907

Hitchcock, *Geology of Massachusetts*, 1841

Howe, M. A. DeWolfe, *Boston Landmarks.* New York: Hastings House, 1947

Howe, M. A. DeWolfe, *Boston Common, Scenes From Four Centuries.* Cambridge: The Riverside Press, 1910

Kilham, Walter H., *Boston After Bulfinch.* Cambridge: Harvard University Press, 1946

King, Moses, *King's Hand Book of Boston.* Cambridge: Moses King Publisher, 1883

Lockwood, Alice, *Gardens of Colony and State.* New York: Scribner, 1931

Mann, Albert W., *Walks and Talks about Historic Boston.* Boston: Mann Publishing Company, 1917

McCord, David, *About Boston.* Boston: Little, Brown Company, 1948

Morrison, Samuel Eliot, *Life and Letters of Harrison Gray Otis, 1765–1848.* Cambridge: The Riverside Press, 1913

Place, Charles A., *Charles Bulfinch, Architect and Citizen.* Boston: Houghton Mifflin and Company, 1925

Quincy, Eliza Susan Morton (Mrs. Josiah), *Memoir of the Life of Eliza S. M. Quincy.* Boston: 1861

Quincy, Josiah, *A Municipal History of the Town and City of Boston, 1630–1830.* Boston: Charles C. Little and James Brown, 1852

Shurtleff, Nathaniel Bradstreet, *A Topographical and Historical Description of Boston.* Richwell and Churchill City Printers, 1891

Snow, Caleb Hopkins, *A History of Boston.* Boston: 1825

Stark, James H., *Antique Views of ye Towne of Boston.* Boston: James H. Stark, 1901

Thwing, Annie Haven, *The Crooked and Narrow Streets of Boston.* Boston: Marshall Jones Company, 1920

Thwing, Walter Eliot, *History of the First Church of Roxbury.* Boston: W. A. Butterfield, 1908

Whitehill, Walter Muir, *Boston, A Topographical History.* Cambridge: The Belknap Press of Harvard University Press, 1959

Winsor, Justin, *The Memorial History of Boston.* Boston: Charles Little and James Brown, 1846

List of Illustrations

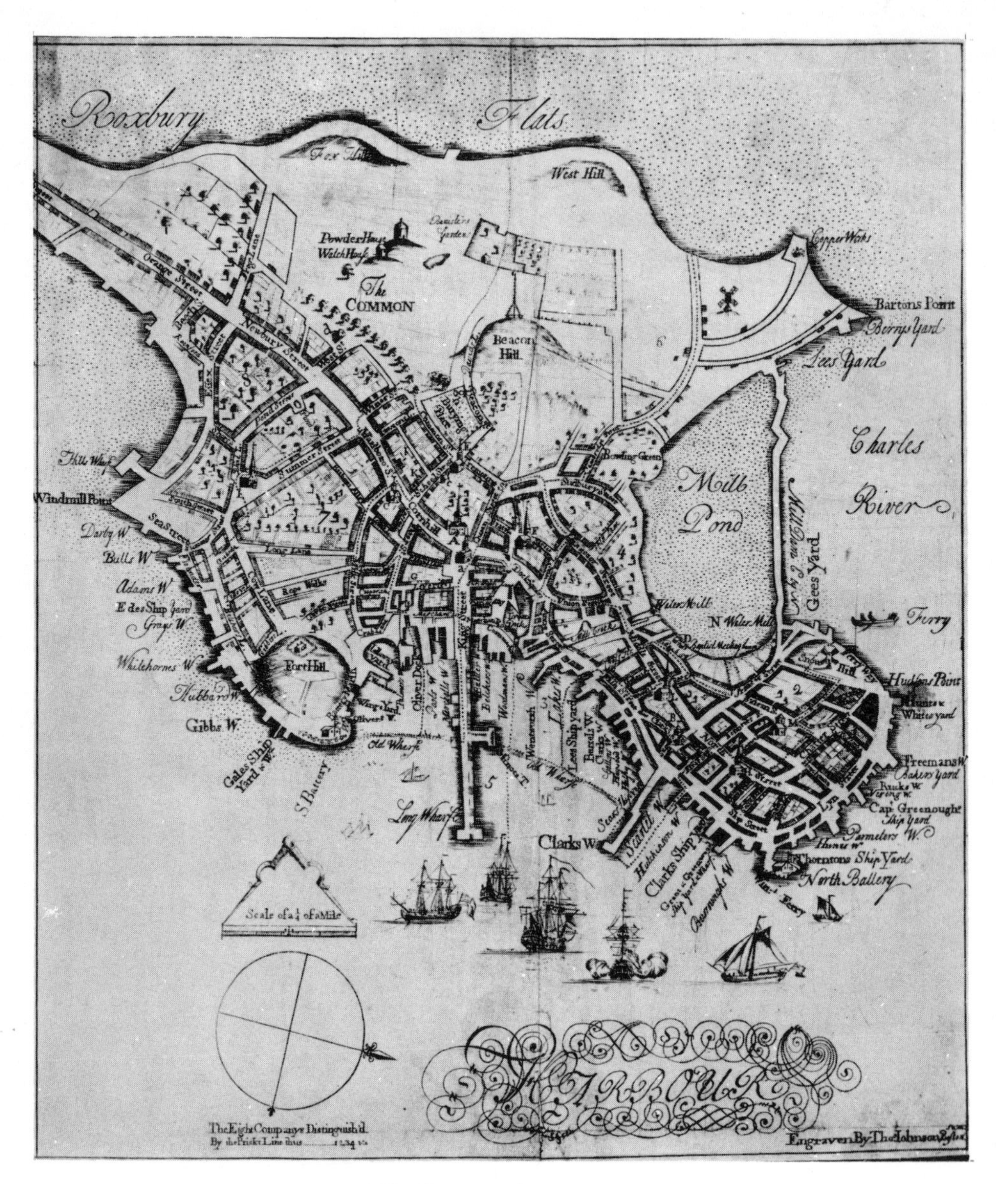

The Burgess Map of 1729

The Book of BOSTON

THE FEDERAL PERIOD 1775 to 1837

Colonial Boston Changes to Federal Boston

BOSTON, so closely allied with the history of the United States, is part of the heritage of all Americans. Founded in 1630 on a tiny peninsula connected by a narrow neck of land to what is now Roxbury, colonial Boston was almost surrounded by water. There were three "mountains" or hills: Copp's Hill, Fort Hill (now leveled), and the Trimountain. The Trimountain had three individual peaks: Cotton (leveled to what is now Pemberton Square), Beacon, where the beacon pole stood (now the State House area), and Mount Vernon (now the Louisburg Square district).*

Colonial life centered in the area of the present State Street, in the North End, and along the water front overlooking the harbor with its many islands. This picturesque Boston was dotted with frame houses built of local wood,

* See Volume I *The Book of Boston — Colonial Boston*, 1630–1775.

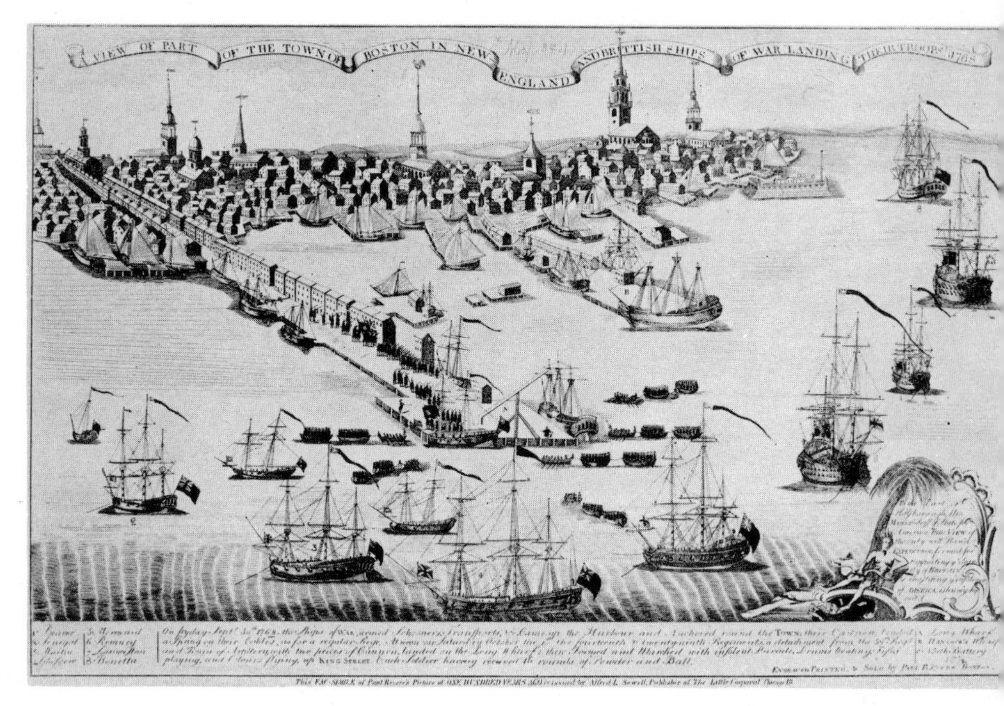

A View of part of The Town of Boston,
printed and sold by Paul Revere, 1768

an American interpretation of the English medieval half-timber style, and some boxlike brick dwellings. All were on small town farms with gardens and orchards. The skyline was pierced with church steeples and the shoreline was fringed with wharves.

As the town grew, land was filled into the harbor, so that the water front was continually changing. Eventually the site of the old Town Dock was about a half mile inland.

Some forty-five acres were set aside for the "common use" and remain so today as Boston Common.

Fires, the horror of those times, gradually brought about the transformation of colonial Boston from a town principally of wooden buildings to one largely of brick.

Up to the time of the War of Independence the colonial

townspeople were puritan in their ideas and standards. Their way of life changed little until the Revolutionary War was over.

England recognized the new nation in 1783. In 1788 Massachusetts ratified the Federal Constitution and in 1789 George Washington was inaugurated as the first President of the United States of America.

A period of readjustment followed, a transition from being a colony to becoming part of an independent nation. There was also an economic depression which was greatly relieved by the development of a new shipping industry and its allied occupations. These days of the late 18th century and the beginning of the 19th century are known as our early Federal period.

At first in the early Federal period new ideas and progress came slowly, but during the first quarter of the 19th century Boston grew rapidly into a charming town of tree-shaded streets and handsome brick homes, producing architecture of a new and beautiful style. People began to "move out to the country," to Beacon Hill * (which is at present near the center of the city,) and the old colonial town farms were replaced by blocks of houses.

Shipping

Shipping increased, and the water front was crowded with sailing ships tied up at the wharves. A forest of masts, silhouetted against the sky, almost concealed the colonial steeples behind them in the town.

* Historic Site.
** Historic Site open to the public.

Horses and wagons clattering along with their loads were hindered by the bowsprits projecting out into the streets, causing "traffic jams" in this busy seaport.

Great wharves were built with brick warehouses and countinghouses to take care of the expanding trade. In 1794 there were eighty of these quays. The most important was the Boston Pier ** or old Long Wharf, at the end of King Street, which had been built in the colonial period and was now greatly lengthened. (See illus. on p. 20.) When King Street became State Street after the Revolutionary War, Long Wharf with its line of buildings extended into the harbor 1,743 feet. In 1800 the sites of Broad and India streets were still under water, but in the next year filling made possible the present India Street, and Central and India wharves were built along the new water front.

Dr. Nathaniel Bowditch (1773–1838), the distinguished scientist and navigator from Boston, made a most valuable contribution to the shipping of his day. Born in Salem, the son of a sea captain, he was apprenticed to a ship chandler and at the age of twenty-one went to sea. His experiences included four long voyages. Although he had no formal schooling after the age of ten, he became a great mathematician, the first in America, as well as an outstanding astronomer. In 1802, before he was thirty, he published his book, *The New American Practical Navigator.* This became a sea captains' manual both here and abroad for more than one hundred years.

There was foreign commerce with Europe and other ports. A vast new East Indies and China trade was developing and there was also shipping to harbors in the West Indies and along the American coast. Both whaling and cod fishery became great industries. Merchants and sea captains amassed

Portrait of Dr. Nathaniel Bowditch by Gilbert Stuart

fortunes from these ships. Some of the voyages made a profit of more than a hundred thousand dollars, an enormous amount of money in those days.

These new merchant ships were threatened by privateers seeking their cargoes, and their captains and men often displayed great courage. One instance of this was commemorated by the presentation of a silver urn to Captain Gamaliel Bradford, a descendant of the Pilgrim governor. This coffee urn, made by Paul Revere, the Boston patriot and silversmith, was engraved, "*To Perpetuate the Gallant defense made by Capt. Gamaliel Bradford in the Ship Industry on 8th July, 1800 — when Attacked by four French Privateers in the Straights of Gibraltar. This urn is Presented to him by Samuel Parkman.*" It is now on view in the ** Museum of Fine Arts, Boston.

Fourteen ropewalks produced the ropes for the many ships. These narrow wooden boardwalks, or roofed sheds

The Bradford silver urn by Paul Revere

with open sides, stretched out in long, straight lines. Myrtle Street on Beacon Hill originally had three ropewalks running from what is now Grove Street to Hancock Street. Others were on the site of the present Pearl Street, on the opposite side of the town, until they burned down. In 1794 the marsh along the water front west of the Common was filled in for a new ropewalk. This remained in use until 1824. Later the area became the Public Garden.

The New England cotton industry developed and supplied the duck and canvas for the sails of the merchant ships. The new American Navy also required sails. Those for the famous frigate *Constitution* were made in the old colonial granary, a large wooden grain storehouse, because no other building in the town was long enough. The granary stood on the site of the present Park Street Church, beside the Old Granary Burying Ground to which it gave its name.

In 1797 the ** U. S. S. *Constitution* was launched, and became our remarkable warship, *Old Ironsides*. She was designed by Joshua Humphries of Philadelphia. Ephraim Thayer supplied the forty-four gun carriages and Paul Revere the copper bolts, screws, and blocks. The figure-head and stern ornaments of stars and a spread eagle were beautifully carved and gilded. This famous sailing ship was built by Edmund Hartt when his yard was privately owned on the site of the Navy Yard.

U.S. Frigate Constitution in the Navy Yard,
painted by Robert Salmon

Old Ironsides, the U.S.S. Constitution, showing the gun carriages

In recognition of his skill Mr. Hartt received a silver tea set made by Paul Revere and engraved, "*Presented by a membership of his fellow citizens as a memorial of their sense of his Ability Zeal and Fidelity in the completion of that ornament of the American Navy 1799.*"

Old Ironsides was so called after she engaged in her well-known encounter with the British *Guerriere* during the War of 1812. This famous sea battle was often portrayed on the mirrors of the day in full color. These paintings on glass were set above the looking-glass panel.

This ship, our oldest man-of-war, is moored today where she was built at the ** Boston Naval Shipyard (established in 1800 in Charlestown) and is visited by thousands yearly. She is one of the many treasures of old Boston.

Across the Charles River from the Navy Yard, at the foot of ** Copp's Hill on Boston's northern shore, were many of the busy shipyards which were building our merchant fleet. Several classes of ships — brigs, schooners, sloops, and later the great square-riggers and the graceful fast clippers — slid down the ways in these and other Boston yards.

The Hartt silver tea set by Paul Revere

Federal merchants' homes on Beacon Street

Doorway at 64 Beacon Street

New Fashions

The new sailing ships brought home cargoes of foreign merchandise. The "China trade" and commerce with other countries in the East supplied a growing demand for oriental goods.

Ivory-handled parasols and canes, fans and sewing gadgets, porcelains, silks, japanned ware of black tin with gold decoration, madras and other cottons, lovely cashmere wool shawls and stoles with bright colored borders were all very fashionable. A sheer white cotton, known as India mull, was also popular. Ladies had dresses, caps, turbans, and long stoles of this transparent gossamer fabric, delicately embroidered in white or color. Curtains of the same material appeared at the windows. In stylish and elegant homes of the early 19th century white mull was often combined with silk in the overdrapery treatments.

Chinese Export porcelain miniature tea set with one full size cup and saucer

French, Louis XVI, andirons of ormolu in the Swan Collection

French materials and other merchandise were also eagerly sought after. Lafayette was popular in Boston and French taste was the fashion. James Swan, a wealthy local merchant engaged in trade with France, sent home to his wife beautiful pieces of furniture, andirons, and candelabra for their new home on Chestnut Street. Many of these treasures are now on display in the Swan Collection at the Museum of Fine Arts.

French chair, c. 1787, in the Swan Collection

English copperplate print cotton, Washington and Franklin, c. 1800

(Left) *Portrait of Mrs. Hephzibah Lord Waterston by Gilbert Stuart, showing a cashmere shawl and mull cap.* (Right) *Portrait of Mrs. John Amory, Jr., by Gilbert Stuart, showing a mull turban*

Luxurious silks, without a pattern, or with the new designs of small flowers or stripes, and of more delicate coloring than the colonial fabrics, were imported for the fashionable classic-style gowns of the Federal ladies.

French copperplate prints on cotton were very much in vogue. These had classic and pastoral designs of rose-red, cobalt blue, or puce on white. There were also English copperplate prints depicting our patriotic heroes, especially Washington and Franklin, surrounded by symbolic goddesses and other classic motifs. These were in great demand in Boston for furniture "covers" and for bed and window hangings. (See illus. on p. 31.)

The portraits of the period, many of which are on view in local collections, display these fabrics. Wives of prom-

(Left) *The Athenaeum Portrait of Martha Washington by Gilbert Stuart, showing a mull cap.* (Right) *The Athenaeum Portrait of George Washington by Gilbert Stuart, used on the dollar bill*

inent citizens were painted in their best dresses of silk or mull with stoles of cashmere or India mull over their shoulders. These new high-waisted, narrow, straight-skirted dresses, so fashionable in France and England in the early 19th century, had replaced the colonial hoop skirts. Most gentlemen had discarded their knee breeches and cocked hats for the new-style long trousers and high-crowned headgear although some, like Paul Revere, still wore "smallclothes."

Many Bostonians of this early Federal period sat for Gilbert Stuart, the great American portrait painter of the time. Several of these paintings may be seen at the Museum of Fine Arts where more than half of Stuart's works are now in the collection.

(Left) *Obelisk tombstone of Benjamin Franklin's parents in the Old Granary Burying Ground.* (Right) *Obelisk tombstone of Chevalier de St. Saveur in King's Chapel Burying Ground*

The head of George Washington painted from life by Gilbert Stuart in 1796 is one of these; it also may be seen at the Museum of Fine Arts where it is on loan from the Boston Athenaeum. This well-known portrait of our first president is now on our one-dollar bills.

Later, after Napoleon had conquered Egypt and Italy, Egyptian and Roman-classic designs were popular. Bostonians followed the French interpretation of these styles. They erected an obelisk monument on Breed's Hill and obelisk tombstones in their graveyards. Other gravestones at this time were surmounted by classic urns.

Ladies embroidered both obelisk and urn memorials, rendered under weeping willow trees in colored silks on white satin. These mourning pictures were very much in favor during this period.

Field canopy bed hung in copperplate print cotton, Mourning Picture over the mantel

Americans slept in "sleigh beds," the French Empire version of the Roman couch. They used smooth Roman columns on their buildings as on the Federal portico of ** King's Chapel.

See *Colonial Boston*, page 99.

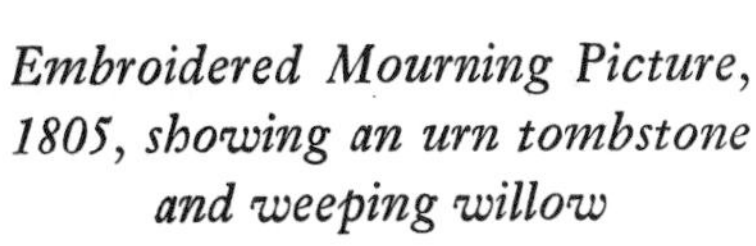

Embroidered Mourning Picture, 1805, showing an urn tombstone and weeping willow

(Left) *Tall clock by Simon Willard, Roxbury c. 1800, with an eagle finial.* (Right) *Wall or banjo clock by Simon Willard, c. 1800, with an eagle finial.*

The eagle, standard of the ancient Romans, became the emblem of the United States. This led to a craze for eagles. They were inlaid in Federal furniture, carved on the crestings of mirrors, cast in brass and placed on the finials of secretaries and tall clocks. Door knockers and the hub decoration of the fanlights of entrance doors, as well as the sterns of ships, were ornamented with gilded spread eagles.

Girandole looking glass, Boston c. 1800, with an eagle finial

Roman motifs were used on our new national silver and gold coins. The ten-dollar gold piece was known as "the eagle." Our silver ten-cent piece is still embossed with the Roman fasces and our twenty-five and fifty-cent pieces also exhibit the eagle. The use of this motif has given rise to the humorous comment that New Englanders are so frugal they hold onto a quarter until the eagle squeals.

Stern ornaments on the U.S.S. Constitution, stars and spread eagle

Fanlight doorway at 61 Beacon Street with an eagle above the door

Liverpool pottery pitcher with an inscription to Boston and another type of jug with a portrait of Captain Hull of the U.S.S. Constitution

Letters conveyed the "latest taste" from abroad to Boston, and orders were sent out with the sea captains from here. Carved white marble mantelpieces were imported from Italy and quantities of china from the East. Merchants living temporarily in England described the British way of life and sent home a variety of movables, including furniture, carpets, glassware, Liverpool and Staffordshire pottery,

Silver pitcher by Paul Revere

Interior of the first Harrison Gray Otis House showing Federal Hepplewhite style chairs and a Hepplewhite-Sheraton style sofa

"setts of tea and coffee china," Sheffield plated ware, and George III silver. Wedgwood and other pottery mantel objects were also highly prized and often were included in the early Federal household inventories.

Liverpool pitchers, jugs of cream-colored pottery with black transfer-printed designs, were common. These often had a portrait of an American hero or ship on one side and American emblems or flags on the other. The shape of these English jugs inspired Paul Revere to make his famous pitcher, here illustrated.

Furniture was of the English Hepplewhite and Sheraton styles, imported or made here by local cabinetmakers. Outstanding among these were Duncan Phyfe of New York and John Seymour of Boston. Boston inventories record "setts of hair bottom chairs" with upholstered seats covered to match other pieces of furniture and curtains in the rooms, or, as they phrased it, "en suite" or "ditto," with the "sopha," "lolling chair," and "window curtains." Many of these beautiful chairs survive in the homes of Boston families and in the local museum collections.

It was a new and elegant age, very different from the early colonial, with classic and oriental influence predominating.

Transportation

As transportation developed, new ideas circulated more quickly. Not only did the sailing ships bring in foreign materials and fashions but inland waterways and canals were dug to stimulate trade in domestic goods to and from Boston. Barges were drawn on these canals by a horse walking along a narrow towpath beside the water. New industries were established and many mills were set up.

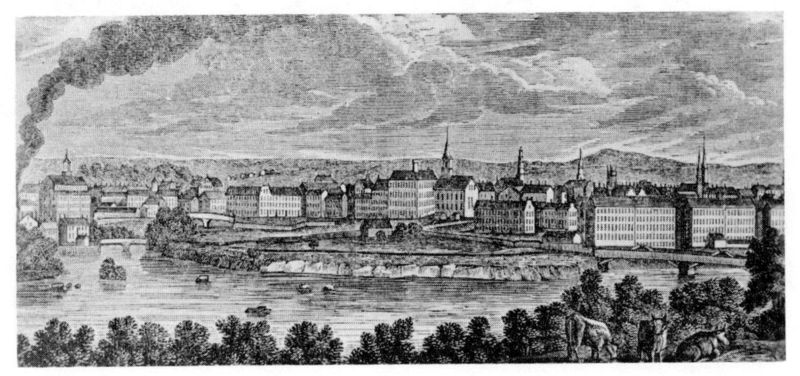

East View of Lowell, Massachusetts, showing the Cotton Mill

Colonel Loammi Baldwin who originated the Baldwin apple also planned the Middlesex Canal. This waterway, incorporated in 1798 and completed in 1804, was of great importance in the development of the cotton industry and later, the granite business.

The course of this waterway, although overgrown and partially lost, may still be traced today, and it is hoped that part of it may be reclaimed, perhaps as a park. This canal, more than twenty-five miles in length, brought boats from Chelmsford and the Merrimack River to Charlestown. The granite for some of Boston's handsome Greek Revival build-

The Middlesex Canal, a reconstructed scene by Louis R. Linscott, showing the Baldwin Mansion in North Woburn and the tow path

BOSTON,

Plymouth & Sandwich

MAIL STAGE,

CONTINUES TO RUN AS FOLLOWS:

LEAVES Boston every Tuesday, Thursday, and Saturday mornings at 5 o'clock, breakfast at Leonard's, Scituate; dine at Bradford's, Plymouth; and arrive in Sandwich the same evening. Leaves Sandwich every Monday, Wednesday and Friday mornings; breakfast at Bradford's, Plymouth: dine at Leonard's, Scituate, and arrive in Boston the same evening.

Passing through Dorchester, Quincy, Wyemouth, Hingham, Scituate, Hanover, Pembroke, Duxbury, Kingston, Plymouth to Sandwich. *Fare*, from Boston to Scituate, 1 doll. 25 cts. From Boston to Plymouth, 2 dolls. 50 cts. From Boston to Sandwich, 3 dolls. 63 cts.

N. B. Extra Carriages can be obtained of the proprietor's, at Boston and Plymouth, at short notice.— STAGE BOOKS kept at Boylen's Market-square, Boston, and at Fessenden's, Plymouth.

LEONARD & WOODWARD.

BOSTON, *November* [illegible], 1810.

(Left) *Boston Mail Stage, 1810.* (Right) *Bell in Hand sign of John Wilson, The Town Crier, hung over his restaurant and later over an alehouse in Pie Alley*

ings was brought from Concord and Chelmsford in this way, or was shipped from Neponset across the harbor after having been hauled from Braintree (now Quincy).

Water was still the easiest means of travel, but more and longer highways were being constructed. New roads such as the Boston Post Road made travel in and out of the town less difficult, although far from comfortable. Stagecoaches carrying passengers and mail were eagerly awaited in the taverns. The first stage left Boston from the Royal Exchange Tavern on King Street (now State Street) in 1772. Regular service followed to several points, and by 1806 the mail went by stagecoach as far as the towns of Albany and New York. It took six days then to reach New York from Boston.

Exchange Coffee House, State Street, 1808–1818, woodcut by A. Bowen

Taverns

Taverns were numerous and continued to be the gathering places where one heard the latest news. *The Bell in Hand Tavern* was established in 1795 by the former town crier, who had rung his bell every hour as he walked the streets and called out, "All is well." The original signboard with the bell and hand painted on it is now in the collection of the Bostonian Society at the Old State House. Some old colonial taverns changed their names to "coffee houses" in the Federal period or took the more popular names of our new patriotic heroes. *The Washington Coffee House* and *The Hancock Tavern* were two of these. The latter, the oldest inn in Boston, situated on Corn Court, a narrow lane near the old Town Dock, had been operated since 1634 as a colonial ordinary. In 1780, when John Hancock became the first governor of the state of Massachusetts, the name was changed to the *Hancock Tavern.* Washington and Franklin had been among the well-known guests. In 1795 Talleyrand stayed here and in 1797 the future King Louis Philippe was a visitor.

As transportation developed and more people came to Boston, there were more and larger hostelries. These were often called "houses" in the early 19th century.

In 1808 the famous *Exchange Coffee House* was built on Congress Street with entrances also on State and Devonshire streets. The great hotel was the largest "house" in the town and Boston's first skyscraper, rising to an unheard-of height of seven stories. Over the center of this brick building was a shallow saucer-like dome of the type which became so popular later in Boston during the Greek Revival period of architecture. Originally the principal floor was intended to be used as a public exchange, but the plan never materialized, as the merchants preferred to continue standing in the street. This circumstance, however, along with the Coffee Room, gave the name to the new hotel. The luxurious interior, in addition to the Coffee Room, included a reading room, a drawing room, a bar, and, on the second floor, a dining room which seated three hundred. Above these were a ballroom, several society rooms, including those of Masonic Lodges, eleven printing offices, and about two hundred bedrooms. Stagecoaches brought notable guests, and many important banquets took place here before the hotel burned in 1818.

Other famous old hotels were the Revere House, the Tremont House, and the Parker House. Only the last named remains in business today. It is well known for its scrod, tripe, and "Parker House rolls."

Bridges

Boston's water-front construction was spreading out like fingers, with wharves and bridges projecting from the tight fist-shaped peninsula that had been colonial Boston. Three of the bridges spanned the ** Charles River. The first, the Charles River Bridge, completed in 1786, connected Boston with Charlestown. This was a splendid wooden toll bridge with a draw in the middle and a wide center lane flanked by railed-off passageways for pedestrians. It was illuminated at night by "forty elegant lamps." A huge crowd assembled for the grand opening which was held on the eleventh anniversary of the Battle of Bunker Hill.

The Devens silver tankard, by Benjamin Burt, engraved with a view of the Charles River Bridge

View of Boston and the South Boston Bridge by J. Milbert, showing the State House

This bridge was recognized as an outstanding engineering feat of the day as shown by one of the gifts presented to those responsible for its construction. A silver tankard, made by Benjamin Burt (1729–1805), was given to Richard Devens, an engineer. On one side was a picture of the bridge and on the other was engraved "*Presented to Richard Devens, Esquire, by the Proprietors of Charles River Bridge in Testimony of their entire Approbation of his faithful Services as a special Director of the Work, begun* A.D. *1785 and Perfected* A.D. *1786*." It may be seen in the Museum of Fine Arts.

The second bridge, the West Boston Bridge, joining Cambridge with Boston, was opened to public travel in 1793. This fine wooden structure stood on the site of the present

Beacon Hill and the Mill Dam

Longfellow Bridge and formed a continuation of Boston's Cambridge Street, affording the most direct route to Harvard College.

In the early 19th century Dorchester Neck was taken over by Boston and another bridge was built to this new area which became known as South Boston. This third wooden bridge, opened in 1805, extended out from the present Dover Street across the South Bay. It became a fashionable promenade and afforded an admirable view of Boston crowned by the new State House.

The Canal Bridge, the third across the Charles River, connecting West Boston to Lechmere's Point in Cambridge, was built in 1809.

Another important engineering feat which facilitated travel out of town was the building in 1814 of the new Mill Dam, west of the city. In 1804 it was voted at a town meeting to fill in the colonial Mill Pond in the North End in order to gain about fifty acres of needed land. (See illus. on

p. 18.) To create new sites for the mills the stone Mill Dam was built across the Back Bay. This ambitious project was one of the many suggested by Uriah Cotting (1766–1819) for the improvement and growth of Boston. A new turnpike, extending from Beacon Street at Charles Street, ran out over the Mill Dam to the hills of Brookline and Brighton and created a second highway from the town, supplementing the old colonial road which followed the Neck to Roxbury.

More Changes

Boston grew slowly immediately after the Revolution, but rapidly in the 19th century. At the time the first census was taken in 1791, there were 18,000 people in the town and 2,376 houses. With the increase in population, the original compact colonial settlement became crowded. New houses were tucked in between the older dwellings on the garden plots and orchards, and the town farms disappeared. These houses seldom faced the street and the ways to them became narrow and often crooked alleys. Soon the old colonial North and South Ends were outgrown.

Beyond these early centers of the town, Summer Street in the new Federal South End and Bowdoin Square in the West End now became the fashionable residential districts. Many prominent old families, however, continued to live in the North End.

The early Federal town gradually became a beautiful and very English Boston of classic red-brick buildings.

Along the new straight streets lots were sold and houses built on them. By 1808 most of these streets were paved with cobblestones brought up from the beaches and laid hit or miss. Some of them may still be seen on Beacon Hill, in Acorn Street, and Louisburg Square. There were a few private street lamps, but as early as 1792 the streets were illuminated by public street lamps. These were cared for by a lamplighter who filled them with whale oil and lit them at twilight.

Some streets were called by the old familiar English names, such as Charles Street, Cambridge Street, and Somer-

Acorn Street, Beacon Hill, showing the original cobblestones and brick sidewalks

Miniatures of Mr. and Mrs. Charles Bulfinch

set Street; but others changed their names after the War of Independence. King Street became State Street, Queen Street was changed to Court Street, and the long road to the Neck, which had been called by four names at various places along the way — Corn Hill, Marlborough, Newbury, and Orange streets — now became Washington Street. Other streets were also called after our American patriots: Hancock, Franklin, Pinckney, and Warren, to mention but a few. The seasons of summer and winter, and trees were also favored names. Beacon Hill still retains Spruce, Willow, Chestnut, and Walnut streets. In 1825 street signs were put up for the first time.

Inadequate water supply caused extensive losses from fire as it had so often during the colonial period. Finally, in 1795, water was brought to Boston through log pipes from Jamaica Pond. Most people, however, were still dependent on wells, pumps, and rain-water cisterns. *The Independent Chronicle*, one of the Boston newspapers, printed advertisements of dwelling houses for sale at this time featuring these conveniences.

Charles Bulfinch

As Boston grew, it was its good fortune to be dominated by the taste of one of America's foremost architects and town officers, Charles Bulfinch (1763–1844). He was New England's first professional architect. His parents were of the colonial aristocracy. The family home, his birthplace, was a three-story gambrel-roofed mansion in Bowdoin Square, built by his grandfather near the present site of the New England Telephone and Telegraph Company building. The houses here had large lawns in front and lovely gardens in the rear. Later, from 1810 to 1815, when blocks of red-brick Federal town houses were built in this area, Bulfinch had his own residence nearby at 8 Bulfinch Place.

After attending the Boston Latin School, graduating from ** Harvard College, and working in a countinghouse, he traveled in Europe for two years. While in France he saw Paris with the Marquis de Lafayette and was very much impressed by the beauty of the town planning there. In 1796 he wrote home to his mother, "Every town in France has one or more public walks shaded with trees and kept in constant repair." ⋆

Returning from abroad in 1787, after what was to him "a highly gratifying tour," ⋆ he "passed a season of leisure, pursuing no business but giving gratuitous advice in architecture."

Devoted to Boston, Bulfinch gave generously of his time, not only in the planning of buildings and streets, but

⋆ *The Life and Letters of Charles Bulfinch, Architect,* by Ellen Susan Bulfinch and the *Autobiographical Sketch* by Charles Bulfinch.

Leveling Beacon Hill, the rear of the State House, and the Bulfinch Monument

also in serving as selectman from 1791 until 1818 when he went to Washington, D.C., to work on the national capitol.

Due to his interest and cultural training, Boston led the country during the early Federal period in the field of architecture and town planning.

On the site of the old colonial beacon that had given the name to Beacon Hill Bulfinch built a * fine monument. This memorial pillar erected in 1790 replaced the beacon blown down the previous year. Erected before the new State House was built or the Hill leveled, this Roman-Doric column of brick covered with stucco stood sixty feet high in a small park that afforded an unbroken view of Boston and the harbor. Set in the base were four tablets depicting the events of the Revolutionary War. The shaft terminated in a beautiful spread eagle now in the Senate Chamber. In 1811, when the peak of the Hill was cut down about sixty feet by the Hancock heirs, the monument was destroyed. In 1899 the Bunker Hill Monument Association set up a replica of the Bulfinch monument near the original site and presented it to the Commonwealth. This is now crowded on all sides by automobiles in a parking lot beside the State House.

The New State House

Bulfinch designed the ** Massachusetts State House on Beacon Street in 1787 but it was not until 1795, two years after John Hancock's death, that the town bought his pasture as the site for the new building. The cornerstone was laid by Governor Samuel Adams and Paul Revere in his capacity as Grand Master of the Grand Lodge of Masons. The stone was drawn to the site by fifteen white horses, one for each state in the Union at that time. The impressive red-brick building with white marble trim, approached by stone steps and set on a turf terrace, was completed in 1798. A letter written by Lord Coleridge (who came to America in 1883) says, "Far the most beautiful city in America so far as I have seen is Boston, and the State House is the most beautiful building in the country — in perfect taste and proportion."

Crowning Beacon Hill, the State House overlooks the Common and dominates Boston. The center of the present

The State House and Boston Common, c. 1830

structure, the red-brick façade, is the original Bulfinch building. The wings were added later when there was need for enlargement. The bricks, painted white in 1825 and yellow later, were restored to the original natural red in 1928. The chimneys were removed when central heating was installed. In spite of these and other changes, much of the old is happily preserved and combined with the new.

The State House by Pendleton, 1830, showing the chimneys

Detail of the State House showing the dome and portico

The dome, the first in Boston, was of wood painted lead color. It was covered with copper by Paul Revere and Sons in 1802, gilded in 1861, and in 1874 the first gold leaf was applied. Blacked out during World War II, the gold leaf has since been replaced and the beautiful dome, terminating in a lantern, shines once more on the Boston skyline.

This noble State House set a fashion for capitol architecture. Previously Bulfinch had designed the State House for Connecticut at Hartford and later, after spending twelve years in Washington, D.C., working on the national capitol, he did the State House for Maine at Augusta. The Boston State House with its superb dome and colonnaded façade is an architectural gem.

The ** interior of the State House, like the exterior, although altered, restored, and enlarged, retains some of the fine original features. Outstanding among these is ** Doric Hall, the beautiful entrance foyer of the Bulfinch front, just inside the Beacon Street door on the first floor. This dignified room, fifty-five feet square, is divided into three aisles by ten noble Doric columns, and is paved with black-and-

Interior of the Bulfinch House, Doric Hall

white marble forming a checked floor. Arched niches frame statues and other memorials of our famous men. The figure of George Washington in white marble, executed by Sir Francis Leggatt Chantrey in 1826, occupies the place of honor in the center. Graceful archways lead to stairways on the east and west. The quiet dignity of this gallery is further enhanced by the whiteness of classic details against a beige wall.

On the second floor the superb Bulfinch interiors remain structurally much as they were in 1798. These rooms now house many paintings, flags, and other objects of historic interest.

Interior of the Bulfinch State House, Senate Chamber showing the ceiling and galleries

Interior of the Bulfinch State House, Senate Reception Room showing the ceiling

The ** Senate Chamber, now used as the Senate Reception Room, is a handsome rectangular apartment with colonnaded ends, like many of the great rooms of this period in England. Here the tall Ionic columns are raised on unusual chamfered bases. Six of the original tall arched windows still light the south and east walls, but those on the north wall were closed when the first addition to the State House was erected. High on the west wall, above the lovely balustraded gallery of the old Senate, is the original clock framed in laurel leaves. The lofty barrel-vaulted ceiling is ornamented with Adamesque detail of white raised plaster on a dark Wedgwood-blue background. The yellow-buff plaster walls are ornamented with the characteristic white classic cornice and pilasters. This is one of the finest examples of the American interpretation of a late Georgian interior in a public building.

The original House of Representatives, ** now the Senate Chamber, is another distinguished room in this style. Directly above the Doric Hall, in the center of the Bulfinch front, it reaches up under the massive dome and is spanned by a great domical ceiling richly decorated with classic raised plaster ornament of white on a background of Wedgwood blue. The spandrels are beautifully decorated with symbolic trophies representing commerce, agriculture, war, and peace. The original woodburning fireplaces, which accented and warmed each corner,. are now gone, but the graceful old colonnaded galleries remain. It is still a superb example of the early Federal-classic style in American civic architecture.

The Council Chamber, now the Governor's Office, occupies the southwest corner of the Bulfinch front. It is twenty-seven feet square with a flat ceiling of white plaster twenty feet high. The smooth plaster walls are of light Wedgwood blue with white Corinthian pilasters, panel mouldings, and other details including the Arms of the State.

Adjoining is the Council Chamber, formerly the Governor's room or private office. From 1798 to 1937 this smaller, simpler room was used by all the chief executives. Originally there were twenty of these minor rooms.

The State House has been added to over the years and many of the newer rooms are good examples of the later periods of architecture.

Among these is Memorial Hall, known as the ** Hall of Flags, a fine circular room with richly colored marbles, mosaics, stained glass, and murals. Here, also, is a splendid display of battle flags and colors.

The ** State Archives, now housed in the newest room (underground), preserve letters and papers of the colonial governors as well as those of George Washington, John Hancock, and others. Here, also, with additional precious material are valuable documents including the original Charter of the Massachusetts Bay Colony of 1628.

The ** State Library, in the Annex, was established in 1828 with 600 volumes and now has more than 750,000. Among its treasures is the original manuscript of Bradford's *History of the Plimoth Plantation.*

The famous codfish known as the ** *Sacred Cod* hangs in the State House in the new House of Representatives at the rear of the Bulfinch building. This emblem of Massachusetts is an interesting old model of a fish, four feet ten inches long, carved from a solid block of pine. It is a colonial replica of an earlier codfish of that period. The original was set up in the Old State House as "a memorial to the impor-

The Sacred Cod

tance of the cod fishery to the welfare of the Commonwealth" and burned there in the fire of 1748. The codfish has always been cherished and cared for as is shown, for example, in a bill from Thomas Crafts, Jr., who charged fifteen shillings to paint it in 1773. At the suggestion of John Rowe, the owner of Rowe's Wharf, it was moved with much ceremony from the old to the New State House in 1798.

New Streets

As early as 1796 Bulfinch had a street plan for Beacon Hill. This was influenced by the tree-shaded squares of London and France with which he was familiar. A park was to extend up the hill on Mount Vernon Street from what is now Willow Street to Walnut. When mansions were built on the ridge they were set back thirty feet from the sidewalk to allow for this garden square which never materialized, but the restrictions on the setback still hold. Much later, however, the well-known Louisburg Square was created nearby, where it remains today, one of the beauty spots of the Hill.

In 1801 Bulfinch became interested in developing the neck to Roxbury. To avoid monotony he laid out streets around an oval grass plot, with the old road, recently renamed Washington Street, running through the center. This park, known as Columbia Square (and later the * Blackstone and Franklin Squares of the Victorian South End), was named for the sailing ship *Columbia.* In 1787 she made the first voyage from Boston to Canton, China, and then continued on to be the first ship to carry the stars and stripes around the world. This took three years. On their return to Boston the men were honored by a dinner given by John Hancock.

India Wharf with the Bulfinch stores and the archway

Wharves and Warehouses

In 1805 Bulfinch designed warehouses, wharves, stores, and streets along the newly made water front, beyond the old colonial South End, flanking Long Wharf at the end of State Street. (See illus. on p. 20.) The India Wharf stores, which preceded India Wharf, formed a long brick block with a central arch. When Atlantic Avenue was cut through, in the Victorian period, it pierced this arch and destroyed all but a few of these fine old stores attributed to him.

Leveling and Filling

As the need for more land continued to press the growing town, a substantial part of the Hill was cut down to fill in along its water front. In 1804 Silas Whitney set up a gravity railroad to speed the progress of grading the west side of the Hill. This railroad, said to be the first of its kind in the country, attracted a great many sightseers. A series of empty cars went up on rails while others went down loaded and dumped the gravel from the top of the "mountain" onto the beach of the Charles River, beyond West Cedar Street, making the land for the present Charles Street area. According to an eyewitness, when Pinckney Street was cut through the top of Mount Vernon it left a bank on the southerly side "thirty or forty feet in height" about opposite the head of Anderson Street. The digging began in another part of the Hill in 1811 at the rear of the State House. Here the dirt was carted away by horses. (See illus. on p. 53.) By 1824 the Hill was leveled to its present height with the exception of Cotton Hill on the east which was not cut down until 1835.

Markets

In 1805 the old colonial ** Faneuil Hall Market was rebuilt and enlarged by Charles Bulfinch into the beautiful building we see today. He doubled the width, added a third story, and moved the cupola forward but reset the original colonial grasshopper weather vane back in its place on the dome. The historic hall on the second floor was also rebuilt by Bulfinch. Here the fine balustraded galleries on the sides,

Faneuil Hall as rebuilt by Bulfinch

supported by columns, and the pilastered walls reflect the classic ornament so popular in this early Federal period. The ground floor continues to be used for a market as it has been for more than two hundred years, a splendid example of a fine old building still serving a useful purpose.

About 1810 Bulfinch built the new Boylston Market on Washington Street near the corner of Boylston, to serve the needs of the growing Federal South End. Parkman's Market in the West End at the corner of Cambridge and Green streets was also built about this time and is attributed by some to Bulfinch. These were of similar design, both being of brick with a cupola, but the Boylston Market was a more notable building. This market, considered 'way out of town at that time, was named for Ward Nicholas Boylston, a liberal benefactor of Boston who gave the clock on its tower. There were twelve stalls accommodating the market on the ground floor and a large hall above. Here in the auditorium, known as Boylston Hall, the famous Handel and Haydn Society, founded in 1816, held concerts for many years. When the building was destroyed the cupola was removed. It may now be seen on the Calvary Methodist Church on Massachusetts Avenue, Arlington.

Interior of Faneuil Hall as rebuilt by Bulfinch

The Boylston Market

Cupola of the Boylston Market now on the Calvary Methodist Church, Arlington

Portrait of Jean Louis A. M. Lefebvre de Cheverus, first Roman Catholic Bishop of Boston

Churches

During the early Federal period Bulfinch built several churches in Boston. The first of these was the Hollis Street Church whose original wooden building had burned along with the neighboring district (now the Metropolitan Theater area) in the great fire of 1787. This church differed in design from his others. The entrance façade had a central pedimented portico and two towers each with a dome. The interior, spanned with a dome ceiling, had a pulpit against the rear wall. This new-style pulpit in front of the congregation was a change from the colonial type located at the side, with a sounding board suspended above, and set a fashion used all over New England in the 19th century. In 1810 this noble edifice was floated down the harbor on a raft to East Braintree.

In 1800 Bulfinch designed without charge the first Roman Catholic Church in New England, for the beloved Bishop Jean-Louis A. M. Lefebvre de Cheverus, an exiled French priest who served as the first Catholic bishop of Boston. Protestants and Catholics alike contributed to the

Church of the Holy Cross, first Roman Catholic Church in New England

building fund. This fine Church of the Holy Cross of red brick with white Italian-classic details was erected in 1803 and razed in 1868. It stood almost at the corner of what is now Franklin and Devonshire streets. The site is marked by a * plaque nearby.

A beautiful French silver coffee urn, made in 1787 in Paris by Mathieu de Machy was presented to Bulfinch in recognition of his services. The engraving reads, "*To Charles Bulfinch, Esquire. Presented by the Catholics of Boston, January 1, 1806.*" It is now in the Museum of Fine Arts.

Bulfinch silver urn by Mathieu de Machy, Paris

Second edifice of the New North Church now St. Stephen's Roman Catholic Church

In 1804 Bulfinch built a handsome church for the "New North Religious Society" on Hanover Street in the North End, across from the present Paul Revere Mall. This is the only one of his Boston churches still standing. Like the Church of the Holy Cross, it is of red brick with white wooden pilasters on the façade, a clock tower, belfry, and an eastern dome, but in other details it differs from the earlier church. The entrance on a projecting porch has a Palladian

St. Stephen's Church, only one by Bulfinch still standing in Boston

window above and higher up a lunette window. Other windows are framed with recessed arches, so characteristic of Bulfinch, and all the windows have rectangular panes of clear glass. Originally there was a Paul Revere bell. This bell and some of the windowpanes have been removed but much of the original church remains.

The simple dignity of the exterior is enhanced by an interior of fine proportions, with two side balconies supported by slender graceful columns. In 1862 it became ** Saint Stephen's Roman Catholic Church. Although some changes were made then, and also when Hanover Street was widened, it remains today a fine example of Bulfinch's ecclesiastical style.

Interior of St. Stephen's Church

Portrait of Asher Benjamin attributed to Chester Harding

Asher Benjamin

Asher Benjamin (1773–1845) was another well-known architect of this early Federal period. Like Bulfinch, he was influenced by the Adam-classic style of the late Georgian period in England. He was perhaps most noted for the numerous books which he published from 1797 to 1841. These were a source of inspiration not only in Boston but throughout New England and served as builders' guides to many. These men built the beautiful classic white wooden homes and churches whose simple dignity is so characteristic of the New England landscape.

Born in 1773, he was ten years younger than Charles Bulfinch and probably was his most serious competitor. Benjamin started his career in the western part of the state.

Later he worked in Connecticut and Vermont. During the years 1826–1828 he made his home in Dunstable, now Nashua, New Hampshire, where he designed the canal locks and helped with the village church, school and street plans. With this exception, he resided in Boston from 1803 until his death in 1845 and designed some notable buildings still standing here today.

West Church by Asher Benjamin

Charles Street Meetinghouse by Asher Benjamin

Outstanding among them is the ** West Church built in 1809, or red brick with a projecting center on the façade and a triple portal. This lovely old Federal church has the usual clock tower with a belfry terminating in a dome which in turn is topped by a weather.vane. White rectangular panel ornaments and pilasters decorate the façade, details used by both Benjamin and Bulfinch, but always in different arrangements. The interior is spacious and dignified, with a handsome ceiling, cornice, and gallery. A beauti-

Detail of the Charles Street Meeting House

ful gilded clock is set in the gallery face above the entrance. The pulpit and the pews were removed in 1892 when it ceased to be a place of worship. We owe the preservation of the West Church to Mr. Andrew C. Wheelwright, who bought the building and maintained it until the city took it over. It was used as a branch of the Boston Public Library from 1896 to 1960. Although threatened during the demolition of the West End, this important church has been saved and will be used for Methodist church services.

Not far away, on what was then the shore of the Charles River, Asher Benjamin built another church in 1807, the ** Charles Street Meetinghouse. Like his West Church, it is of brick with a projecting porch and terminates in a tower with a belfry, a dome with a weather vane, and a clock which still strikes the hours. This style of clock tower was a popular feature in the Federal period, but each was of different design. Bulfinch and Benjamin used a variety of domes on top of their clock towers instead of spires. Both of Benjamin's Boston churches have the classic features of the period — pilasters, panel ornaments on the façades, and arched sashed windows set with rectangular panes of clear glass. The Charles Street Meetinghouse also has arched doorways framing fanlighted doors, a balustrade with urn finials, and a cupola completely different from that on his West Church. Although both have been much altered in their interiors, these beautiful meetinghouses have been little changed externally. Boston is most fortunate in having these two Benjamin churches at the foot of Beacon Hill, one on Cambridge Street near Bowdoin Square and the other on lower Mount Vernon Street at the corner of Charles Street.

Peter Banner, an Englishman, who worked in Boston from 1806 to 1828, built the ** Park Street Church in 1809, on the corner of Park and Tremont Streets overlooking the Common. The graceful white steeple of this brick church is one of the highest and finest of its type in Boston. Seen through the trees by day and under modern illumination at night, it is a thing of beauty. Originally it was higher, but after a great gale which caused it to sway, it was rebuilt with some changes by the architect Gridley J. F. Bryant (1816–1889).

Park Street Church by Peter Banner

Detail of the Park Street Church

The bowed columned sections flanking the entrance to the church are unusual and stately. The fine capitals of the columns were executed by Solomon Willard (1783–1861), a carver of distinction.

This church stands on the site of the old colonial granary, a spot later known as "Brimstone Corner" because gunpowder was stored in the church basement during the War of 1812. Here at the Park Street Church William Lloyd Garrison spoke convincingly against slavery and in 1832 the song "America" was first sung — to mention but two of the important events of its past.

Meeting House Hill, Roxbury, 1790, from a painting by John Ritts Penniman

On Meeting House Hill in Roxbury stands the ** Eliot Church, the oldest wooden meetinghouse left in Boston. Built in 1804, this typical New England white church, with clear, small-paned windows and green blinds, a bell made by Paul Revere and a clock on the steeple, crowns this historic area. It is named for the early colonial pastor, John Eliot, who preached to the Indians in their own language. Later, during the Revolutionary War, George Washington viewed the towns of Boston and Charlestown through a spyglass from this vantage point.

The church records reveal the changes in the way of life here through the years. The parishioners of this early Federal period were engaged in many professions and businesses, indicative of the diverse interests of Boston. Among them were schoolteachers, lawyers, and physicians; merchants dealing in dry goods, flour, wool, cotton, and the China trade; shopkeepers, tanners, farmers, blacksmiths, gardeners, ropemakers, master mariners, soap boilers, candlemakers, coopers, and bankers. In 1790 there was a row of horse sheds with arched openings for the use of those driving from a distance to church. In 1820 the church was warmed by two woodburning stoves, the first heat in the building.

State Street, 1792, showing the old State House

Other Red-Brick Buildings

There were other notable buildings of brick in Federal Boston. Many were designed by Bulfinch, among them the Boston Bank on State Street and the new Almshouse built on Leverett Street overlooking the Charles River. This long three-story edifice, built in 1799, had a higher center unit, accenting the façade, and a basement kitchen, a feature which became popular in Boston during the Victorian period.

View of State Street, 1830–40, by Bartlett showing columned buil

ngs, center right, the U.S. Bank, and far right, the Suffolk Bank

Silver urn by Paul Revere with engraving of the First Boston Theater by Bulfinch

The First Boston Theater

At the corner of Franklin and Federal streets stood the first Boston theater. Built in 1794, it was indicative of the new way of life in Federal Boston. Gone was the old Puritan attitude of frowning on pleasure. The theater was eagerly desired and greatly admired. Bulfinch designed this splendid building without charge and supervised the construction. Unfortunately it burned in 1798 and the beautiful exterior

First Boston Theater as rebuilt by Bulfinch with the Tontine Crescent at the left

is known to us only as pictured on a gold medal presented to him, and also on a silver urn made by Paul Revere, and in other engravings. It was speedily rebuilt with a plainer façade but with a rich interior. There was a spacious ballroom as well as a theater, retiring rooms, and a kitchen. The handsome circular auditorium had a color scheme of azure blue, lilac, and straw color, accented with gold, and the boxes were hung with crimson silk.

This pleasant neighborhood with its beautiful churches and dwelling houses was later swallowed up either by commercial enterprises or in the great Boston fire of 1872.

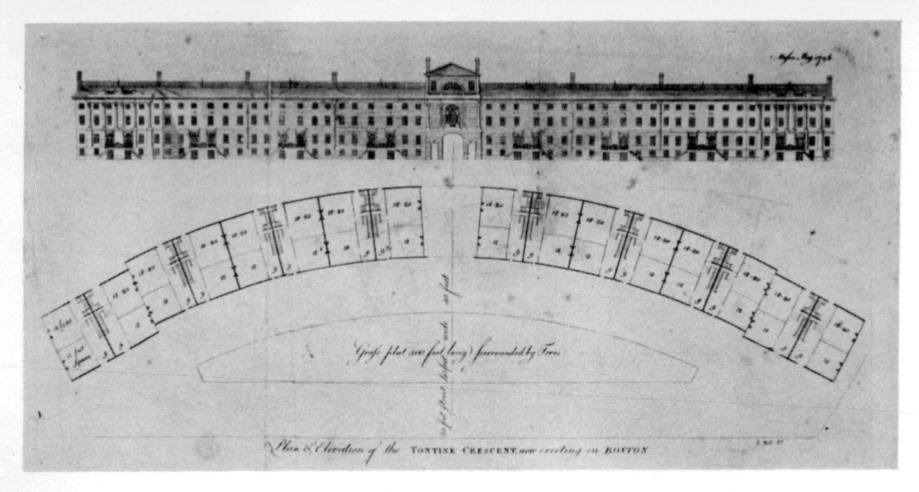

Plan and Elevation of the Tontine Crescent by Bulfinch

Residences

Many of Boston's most beautiful homes were built before the War of 1812 and its attending financial difficulties. Several of these were free standing, as they were in the colonial period, but most of the Federal houses in the town were attached and formed blocks or rows along the new straight streets. Brick sidewalks were laid when the houses were built and shade trees were planted. The houses were mostly of brick with slate roofs, but a few were still of wood, and some at the end of the period were of granite. They were of all sizes, including a surprising number of three or more story mansions built by wealthy merchants of the day. Many of these handsome early Federal residences still remain standing on Beacon Hill or tucked away among later and taller buildings in the older parts of the city.

Boston is unique in this picturesqueness. Few other cities in the country have so many examples of the old rosy-brick architecture which reflects so clearly the gracious living of the early days of our republic. These fine old houses are worthy of study as representative of the best in American taste.

The Tontine Crescent at the right of the Park and Franklin Place houses at the left, Franklin Street 1794

The Tontine Crescent

The * Tontine Crescent was the first and most beautiful block of houses in Boston. Built in the fashionable new South End in 1793, it was designed by Bulfinch. The name Tontine Crescent came from the method of financing and the crescent shape of the buildings. The money was to be obtained by selling shares of stock in this project. This was offered to the public, but only half the shares were sold and William Scollay, Charles Bulfinch, and his brother-in-law Charles Vaughn assumed the rest of the financial obligation. The garden and pastures of Joseph Barrell behind his residence on Summer Street were purchased and a range of brick houses five hundred feet long was erected on Franklin Street

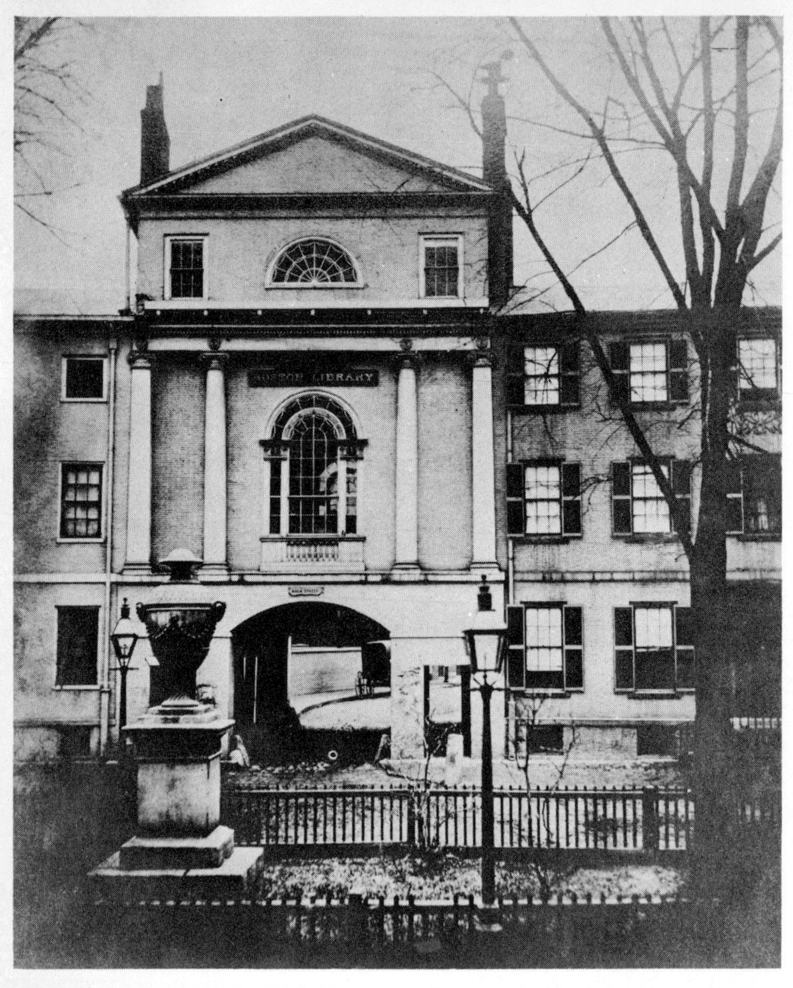

Detail of the center of the Tontine Crescent showing the archway with the street sign, Arch Street, and the Franklin Urn

where the street still bends. This handsome curved row of sixteen individual homes, so like those of Bath, England, was designed as one building or unit. Originally there were to be two of these crescents facing each other across an oval park, but owing to some difficulty in obtaining the land, the second block was built in a straight line and called Franklin Place. (See illus. on p. 89.)

Here large mansions were erected, in four groups of double or twin houses. These sold for $8,000 each, a high price in those days before electricity, plumbing, and central heating. They were handsome, with the characteristic Bulfinch features, such as recessed arches framing the first-floor windows and pilasters on the façade above. Later a projecting enclosed entrance porch or vestibule was added. This became popular on both large and small houses all over New England. These fine homes were of brick painted gray. The painting of brick houses, perhaps to make them more weatherproof, is thought to have been introduced by Bulfinch at this time.

The center of the Tontine Crescent was higher and emphasized by an arch spanning a passageway, now ** Arch Street. Above this archway were the rooms of the Massachusetts Historical Society and the Boston Public Library. Part of the center section with pilasters and a Palladian window was later reproduced and may be seen at number 18 Milk Street at the end of Sewall Place, a small byway.

The grassy tree-shaded park in front of the Tontine Crescent, three hundred feet long, was enclosed by an iron railing and had a large classic urn set up in the center in memory of Benjamin Franklin. This was brought from England by Bulfinch and now stands over his grave in Mount Auburn Cemetery, Cambridge.

It is a great loss to Boston that the Tontine Crescent, so important in American architecture, is gone, but more than that, it is a great pity that this artistic venture should have been the cause of the financial ruin of the Bulfinch family. The withdrawal of his partners, due to the economic stress of the times, forced him into bankruptcy and a term in jail for debt. This distinguished gentleman, who did so much for Boston and the architecture of his country, deserved a better fate.

Pearl Street showing the Richardson and Harris Houses at the corner of High Street

Other Brick Houses in the Federal South End

Near the Crescent the streets leading off Washington Street to the harbor on the south and the Common on the north were also residential. Here on Essex Street Gilbert Stuart, the well-known American portrait painter, made his home from 1806 until he died in 1828. These quiet streets were lined with blocks of brick town houses joined together. Some were uniform but not designed as one building, like the Crescent. In addition there were detached mansions with gardens and fine stables of classic design in the rear. All were close to the new brick sidewalks. Most of the houses had iron railings and many had small balconies of iron wrought with delicate classic motifs. Shade trees were planted along the streets and in the yards at the rear of the houses, lindens

Portrait of Thomas Handasyd Perkins, c. 1827, by Gilbert Stuart

and elms being the favorites. Summer Street was one of the loveliest of these streets. No one realized then that this quiet residential section later in the same century would become the shopping center of a great city.

Farther on, toward the water and on Fort Hill, now leveled, were more handsome homes. On tree-shaded Pearl Street were many large free-standing mansions, among them the residences of Jeffrey Richardson, Jonathan Harris, Josiah Quincy, James Perkins and his brother Thomas Handasyd Perkins. The latter, a leading merchant who traded in China and Java, had a fine home at number 17 with a double stair leading to the front door, a gate for carriages to drive in, and the usual courtyard and stable in the rear. Here Lafayette sent his son, George Washington Lafayette, to live with his friend Colonel Perkins during the French Revolution. In 1833 Perkins moved to a bow-front house on Temple Place, now incorporated in the Provident Institution for Savings, and gave his Pearl Street home to the Institute for the Blind, which still bears his name.

Colonnade Row, by Bulfinch, from the Common
Design on the cover of the music Promenade Quick Step, 1843, showing the Tremont Street Mall

Colonnade Row

Opposite the south side of the Common, looking to tree-shaded Tremont Street Mall and the Charles River, stood a row of stately homes built in 1810 and attributed to Bulfinch, known as Colonnade Row. These nineteen attached town houses, now replaced by stores, stretched from West to Mason streets on Tremont Street and had a Doric colonnade supporting a delicate iron balcony under the long drawing-room windows of the second floor. The elderly Dorothy Quincy Hancock, then widowed and remarried to Captain James Scott, lived here and stood in the window to wave to her old friend Lafayette as he passed by during his visit to Boston in 1825.

Park Street Residences

In the early 19th century the old colonial Sentry Lane that led up to Sentry or Beacon Hill was straightened and paved to become the residential Park Place, later called ** Park Street. Here at the corner of Beacon Street, opposite the new State House, Bulfinch built a large four-story mansion for Thomas Amory in 1804. Part of this handsome brick dwelling house still stands, although it is defaced by stores. On the Park Street side, at the right of the façade on the first floor, are some of the original windows framed in arched recesses. One half of the entrance portico of stopped fluted columns with carved details in the flutes remains with its splendid stone "horseshoe stair" and graceful curved iron

Armory-Ticknor House on the left and Park Street Mall on the Common at the right

railing. Still unimpaired at the foot of the steps is a beautiful Adamesque street lamp of the type so popular in London at this time. This great town house has received many distinguished visitors, among them Lafayette, who lodged here in 1825 when he came to Boston to take part in the dedication of the Bunker Hill Monument. In 1830 Professor George Ticknor bought the mansion and installed his famous library, one of the best in Boston.

With proper restoration this house would make an ideal governor's mansion today, not only because it is one of the few Bulfinch residences left to us, but also because it is convenient to the State House and large enough for a governor's family and the necessary entertaining.

In addition Bulfinch built a row of four uniform houses on Park Street in 1805. These attached town houses had his usual characteristic arched recesses framing the ground-floor windows, and there was also a long wrought-iron balcony of classic detail under the drawing-room windows. Number 4, now the site of the Paulist Fathers Catholic Information Center, was the last to go, in 1956.

Bowdoin Square

The West End, around Bowdoin Square at the foot of Beacon Hill, was another fashionable area being built up at this time. There were blocks of attached brick houses as well as unattached mansions along the new streets. This part of the town where Bulfinch was born was also the birthplace of another prominent Bostonian, Harrison Gray Otis (1765–1848). Descended from a long line of lawyers, he was unable to go to London to study law after his graduation from Harvard, as the Revolutionary War had ruined his father financially. In 1780 he wrote to Samuel Breck "that the utmost extent of his desires as to riches was to be worth $10,000." In 1786 he had nothing, but fourteen years later, before he was thirty-five, he was rich. He had become a successful lawyer and made a fortune in real-estate investments.

At the corner of Cambridge and Lynde streets he built the ** first of his magnificent homes, all designed by Bulfinch. This large three-story house resembles a drawing by

First Harrison Gray Otis House now the Headquarters of the Society for the Preservation of New England Antiquities

Bulfinch in his sketchbook and a similar one, done in color, found among the Otis papers. Built in 1797, beside the West Church, it is of brick with a Venetian or Palladian window over the entrance and a lunette window on the floor above, an arrangement Bulfinch also used on St. Stephen's Church.

Interior of the first Harrison Gray Otis House by Bulfinch –
The Dining Room

The sash windows are rectangular, having the small panes set six over six, except on the third floor where the windows are shorter, almost square, as is usual in these houses. The entrance steps are of stone, as are the keystoned window lintels. The original cornice, of which one section remains, was of wood and is to be restored around the entire façade. The graceful semicircular entrance porch is a later addition probably dating from about 1810.

The interior is spacious and has the usual plan of the period. On the ground floor at the right is the front parlor, on the left the dining room, with the kitchen in the rear. Above are the drawing room, the front chamber, and other bedchambers. The servants' sleeping rooms were on the top floor. The fine entry or entrance hall is in the center of the house. Here a straight flight of stairs with delicate urn turned and twisted balusters leads to the second floor only. This grand staircase is lit by the fan and side lights of the entrance door and by two Palladian windows, one on each landing on the front and rear of the upper hall. The back stairs rising to the top of the house around a rectangular well are simpler in design with round newels and plain square balusters. Such an arrangement of two staircases is often found in these town houses.

The dining room is well known for its superb woodwork with carved classic details in white on an Adam-green background, and is an outstanding example of the delicate late Georgian style of Bulfinch's domestic interior finish.

Restoration was necessary in order to bring this important early Federal house back to its original dignity, for, like so many other beautiful old buildings, it was allowed to deteriorate as the neighborhood changed. It was defaced by shops and their trade signs, including a Chinese laundry and a "Ladies' Turkish Bath," and the upper floors were used as a rooming house. In 1916 the Society for the Preservation of New England Antiquities acquired the property as its headquarters and it is now restored and appropriately furnished. It is open to the public for a small fee which includes a visit to the ** museum attached to the rear of the house. Here there is a splendid collection of architectural fragments, decorative arts and crafts. Here, also, is a large collection of photographs showing exteriors and interiors of New England homes and other buildings.

Beacon Hill

In 1795 a group of prosperous people, including Bulfinch and Otis, formed a syndicate called the "Mount Vernon Proprietors." They purchased the colonial farm lands of the portrait painter, John Singleton Copley, after he moved to England, and began to transform Mount Vernon, the southwest slope of Beacon Hill, into another new residential district. In 1799 streets were laid out and lots sold. The colonial pastures and blueberry bushes disappeared as the Hill developed. Between 1806 and 1812 fifteen houses were built on the old Copley land. Earlier houses had been built by some of the Mount Vernon Proprietors for their own use and probably to stimulate building in the neighborhood as well.

One of the first of these houses was the second mansion designed by Bulfinch for Harrison Gray Otis. Built in 1802 on Olive Street, on the ridge of the Hill, now * 85 Mount Vernon Street, it is set back thirty feet from the street with a lawn in front. This pretentious, free-standing brick town house has the usual white classic trim. It retains much of the proper setting and is still a private residence. There have been few outward changes except for the entrance, which has been moved from the west front to the east, and the addition of a bowed room which projects on the west. The main entrance

Second Harrison Gray Otis House by Bulfinch

on the side opening onto the cobblestone carriageway was a new idea at this time in Boston and is thought to have been introduced by Bulfinch. The stately street façade, differing markedly from the first Harrison Gray Otis house, shows Bulfinch's versatility. The four long embrasured sash win-

Detail of the Second Harrison Gray Otis House

dows open onto wrought-iron balconies of Chinese fretwork design. White wooden Corinthian pilasters which ornament the upper stories accent the façade. All the windows have stone lintels and the new slat blinds which were just coming into fashion. Above the cornice is a roof rail and on the roof

Third Harrison Gray Otis House by Bulfinch

is a chamfered cupola. Both of these new features soon became characteristic of the larger New England mansions. Many sea captains' and merchants' houses had these glazed cupolas from which they watched for their returning ships. Several may still be seen on Beacon Hill. The interior, although altered, retains some of the original features.

Detail of the third Harrison Gray Otis House

In 1806 Mr. Otis built his * third mansion designed by Charles Bulfinch. This was his home until his death forty years later. Here he entertained many notable people including President Monroe, who came for a New England Thanksgiving dinner in 1817. This great house stands on its original site at 45 Beacon Street on the down slope of the

Hill, overlooking the Common. It is one of the few in Boston with its stable unchanged nearby. The four-story house of brick with white trimmings has stone lintels over the windows on the upper floors and wooden cornices above the long sash windows of the drawing room on the second floor. These windows open onto wrought-iron balconies of interesting design, combining the two accents of the period, classic and oriental, in the Greek key and Chinese fret detail, which is repeated in the railings along the street and on the entrance-porch roof. There are two entrances, the front on the street and the other opening onto the cobblestone carriage driveway at the side, both with rectangular porticoes and stone steps. The house is unchanged on the exterior except for the ground floor, where a granite basement was added later, and the bow end on the east was obliterated in 1831 when Otis built another house (now number 44 Beacon Street) for one of his daughters, Mrs. Ritchie, on the garden lot. (See illus. on p. 165.)

The tree-shaded yard and the old stable are still there. This stable has the arched doors and fine proportions which make these Federal buildings so important architecturally.

The interior is completely changed, leaving no hint of its former beauty. Originally the oval room, of which only a part remains, formed the bow end on the garden side. The fine interior finish is also gone, but the stories of the gay social life of the early 19th century here live on. Quantities of food were always on hand for Otis's family of eleven children and the many friends who came in and out. It was said that every afternoon a ten-gallon blue-and-white Lowestoft punch bowl was filled and placed on the landing halfway up to the drawing room for the refreshment of these visitors. This stately house is now used and well cared for by the present owners, the American Meteorological Society.

Stable and Yard of the third Harrison Gray Otis House

87 Mount Vernon Street

Other houses on the Hill are attributed to Bulfinch or reflect his taste. Outstanding among these is the mansion at * 87 Mount Vernon Street built by Stephen Higginson, Jr., now the headquarters of the Colonial Society of Massachusetts.

The Higginson family were loyal Federalists and prominent Bostonians. Stephen Higginson, Senior, a wealthy merchant and former sea captain, moved here from Salem in 1778. He was influential in establishing our Navy Yard at Charlestown, across the Charles River from Boston. Like many boys of those days who went to sea in their teens and were sea captains in their early twenties, he made many voyages and acquired a wide experience.

Also like many other Americans of these days, he traveled abroad and was familiar with the "latest taste." In 1800 and again from 1806–1812 he lived in London, and the last two of his three wives were British, the daughters of a wealthy merchant. His Boston residence from 1811–1828 was at 49 Mount Vernon Street.

His son, Stephen Higginson, Jr., also lived graciously. His home in Boston from 1807–1810 was the large brick attached town house adjoining 89 Mount Vernon Street. These dwellings were built at the same time and may have been twin houses, but number 89 now is completely changed. The Higginson house purchased from Bulfinch retains much that is original, including the arched recesses framing the ground-floor windows, the stone upper-window lintels, and the wooden cornices above the long windows on the second floor, also found on the Amory-Ticknor and the third Otis houses. Set high on the Hill with a stable in the rear, it is approached by a graceful, curved cobblestone carriageway which is still in use today.

The interior plan is characteristic of these town houses. The front parlor is on one side of the entrance and the dining room on the other, with the kitchen in the rear equipped with a wide cooking fireplace and the usual brick oven. The entry or center hall retains the fine circular stair winding to the fourth story and lit by a roof-light above set with radiating panes of clear white glass.

A brick house built in 1804 (now 55 Mount Vernon Street) is also attributed to Bulfinch but is probably the work of Asher Benjamin. Although altered, it is noteworthy for the entrance on the side without a carriageway, the brick cornice, and window embrasures.

On Chestnut Street there are three beautiful attached town houses, now numbers * 13, 15, and 17, built in 1806 and attributed to Bulfinch. These were purchased by Mrs. Hepzibah Swan and, later, given to her daughters when they married. Mrs. Swan, the only woman among the Mount Vernon Proprietors, was the wife of Colonel James Swan, previously mentioned on page 30. These fine houses have been somewhat altered but still have many original details. The entrance doorways, set in a rectangular recess and placed at the side of the façade, are flanked by slender fluted Doric columns under a wide lintel, and the long drawing-room windows open onto individual bowed balconies of delicately wrought iron.

All three houses originally had brick stables in the rear. These were of two levels because of the slope of the hill, with the horse stalls on the ground floor and the * carriage house above. This upper floor opened onto Mount Vernon Street and may be recognized today, although it is now re-built into one-story homes. They can never be more than thirteen feet high due to a restriction in Mrs. Swan's deeds to her daughters. The deeds also provide for the preservation of an inclined pathway, eight feet wide, through which the

13, 15, 17 Chestnut Street

Doorway of 17 Chestnut Street

horses were formerly brought up from the stableyard to the carriage house. One of these houses, now number 60 Mount Vernon Street, was for many years the studio of Mrs. Swan's great-granddaughter.

The interiors of numbers 13, 15, and 17 Chestnut Street had spacious double parlors divided by archways with doors. These rooms were enriched with beautiful mantels and delicately reeded door and window trims. Number 17 still has the superb circular staircase with the slender carved balusters and sweeping handrail. After being in the Swan family for generations, this house has today been made into apartments.

Portrait of Colonel James Swan by Gilbert Stuart

Elegant furnishings sent home by Colonel Swan adorned these town houses of his daughters' and his wife's two residences. Mrs. Swan spent the winters at 16 Chestnut Street and went to her country house in Dorchester on May first. Much of this French furniture and some of the *objets d'art*, after being in 17 Chestnut Street for many years, are now on view in the Museum of Fine Arts.

Judge Tudor, whose winter home was on Court Street and summer place in Saugus, was another Bostonian of note. His two sons made names for themselves in very different ways. William began in 1811 the publication of *The North*

American Review, which became one of the leading periodicals. He also was one of the founders of the Boston Athenaeum, established in 1808. This private library was located at 13 Pearl Street in 1822, in the mansion generously donated by Mr. James Perkins. The Athenaeum also housed the American Academy of Arts and Sciences which had been founded in 1791. Both of these distinguished institutions are making important intellectual contributions today.

Frederick Tudor, William's brother, to the amazement of his friends, made a fortune selling New England ice in

Blue Staffordshire printed ware plate with a view of the James Perkins House on Pearl Street given by him to the Boston Athenaeum

Boston Common to the State House, 1815–20, by J. R. Smith showing the Frederick Tudor House fourth from the left, the Armory-Ticknor House on the right and the cows on the Common

the West Indies. He purchased the Thorndike house on the corner of Beacon and Joy streets, now the site of the Tudor Apartments, for his residence. This stately mansion had a large cupola on the roof commanding a view of the harbor. Undoubtedly from here he watched his ships set sail for the tropics with their cargoes of ice. (See illus. above.)

Many of the best examples of Beacon Hill homes are in run-down neighborhoods not yet reclaimed.

The fine double house at * 26 Allston Street, built in 1811 by Cornelius Coolidge, is one of these. It serves as an apartment house now, but the exterior still has its original well-proportioned brick façade and graceful iron railing framing the stone double stairway which leads to the second-floor entrances.

Double house at 26 Allston Street

There were other architects working on the Hill together with good housewrights and builders. The construction of the houses was solid and the craftsmanship good in these early Federal days. The house at 74 Pinckney Street, now the home of the author, was designed by the architect John Kutts and built by Weeks and Perrin. This small brick house of three-and-a-half stories, built in 1829, is unusual in that there is an agreement filed with the deed noting the type of construction (to include a brick sidewalk), the prices of wallpapers (some with borders), the black marble mantelpieces, and other details. The interior still remains for the most part as it was built, with the circular staircase in the entry leading to the second floor and the rectangular rear staircase winding to the top of the house (both with plain round balusters), the inside shutters and outside slat blinds on the windows, two beautiful Wyatt windows, all five fireplaces with their mantelpieces, and the Prussian-blue front and rear doors.

Wyatt window at 74 Pinckney Street

Behind this house, approached by a narrow brick passageway, is the * "Hidden House" — so called because it is not on any street. This tiny house was built on a field in the rear of 74 Pinckney Street and is now completely surrounded by larger brick homes.

On some streets there are groups of houses with similar architectural details. There are several * Wyatt windows on West Cedar Street and beautiful entrance doors deeply * recessed in archways on Chestnut Street.

Chestnut Street houses showing the recessed arched doorways

9 West Cedar Street, home of Asher Benjamin

A range of houses on West Cedar Street, with a long iron balcony of classic detail extending under the second-floor drawing-room windows, is attributed to Asher Benjamin. His own home, now number * 9, built in 1833, was one of these. Inside, rising from the entry to the top of the house, is the original staircase curving around an oval well. The smooth round balusters encircle the lower newel post and on the handrail above is a "peace button" of mushroom shape. These were frequently found on the stairways of this period and were supposed to symbolize the fact that the house was satisfactory, the bill paid, and the builder and the owner at peace.

Twin houses, 54 and 55 Beacon Street, by Asher Benjamin

Detail of 54 and 55 Beacon Street

In 1808 a young merchant, James Smith Colburn, built the beautiful brick twin houses opposite the Common which are now * 54 and 55 Beacon Street. The former was for his sister's family and the latter for his own. These bow-front residences designed by Asher Benjamin were among the first of this type in Boston where the swell-front style was to become very characteristic of the town houses.

They are adorned on the ground floor with a colonnade of slender fluted Doric columns supporting a balcony of delicate ironwork under the long windows of the drawing rooms above. The upper façade is decorated with white wooden pilasters terminating in a rich cornice and a roof rail. Smaller balconies of the same ironwork accent the upper stories connecting the balanced curves of the façade, and two "lanthorn" or dormer windows light the garret of each house. The fanlighted entrances have side lights to the floor and are placed in the center of this double façade. At one time these stately brick mansions were painted yellow with white trim. Within are oval dining rooms on the ground floor with drawing rooms above and bedchambers in the upper stories. These were among the first oval rooms in Boston and are among the few surviving in the city today.

The early history of these buildings is documented in the personal memoirs of the original owner, Mr. Colburn. He records, "They were planned by myself and the work executed by A. Benjamin, architect." Later in 1808, after he remarried, he writes: "We went immediately home to my new house in Beacon Street, which I had furnished with elegant furniture. . . . We had a great deal of dinner company, balls, etc. and lived in a fashionable style, as I could well afford it, for I was then worth over half a million dollars." He was twenty-eight years old at this time and had made his entire fortune in ten years since setting out for London with only $1,000, $200 of which was spent for the passage!

In 1845 Number 55 Beacon Street became the home of William H. Prescott, the great American historian, who lived there until his death in 1856. Here he wrote the *Conquest of Peru* and entertained distinguished guests from all

Portrait of Mrs. James Smith Colburn by Gilbert Stuart

over the world, among them William Makepeace Thackeray. These famous houses, such noteworthy examples of the work of Asher Benjamin, are being carefully preserved. Number 54 is an apartment house and number 55 became in 1944 the Headquarters House of The National Society of the Colonial Dames of America in the Commonwealth of Massachusetts.

To leave the Hill momentarily, the * Commandant's House (1809), overlooking the water front at the Charlestown Navy Yard, is another of these early double bow-front houses. Although completely altered inside and out, this fine

The Tea Party by Henry Sargent
Interior of the artist's home at 10 Franklin Street c. 1820

The Dinner Party by Henry Sargent.
Interior of the artist's home at 10 Franklin Street c. 1820

house with a double swell front is still in use and may be seen from the approach to the Mystic River Bridge, along with a fleeting glimpse of the Navy Yard and *Old Ironsides.*

On Beacon Hill there are many other notable houses too numerous to mention in this small volume. Every street is lined with these charming old brick residences.

The interiors on the Hill have often been altered, but many fine staircases, cornices, dadoes, mantelpieces, door and window mouldings are still intact. Letters of travelers, paintings, and inventories of the period reveal the furnishings and color schemes of these gracious rooms. Most of the houses had wallpaper then, and the woodwork was painted white or gray. Floors were covered with handsome carpets or painted floor cloths. There were colorful overdraperies of rich materials, often festooned, trimmed with ball or tassel fringes, and caught up with elaborate cords and tassels. Satin was the most popular fabric for the formal rooms. Colors were brilliant, and there was a great deal of emerald green, azure blue, lilac, crimson, puce, and yellow. "Parlors" usually had a "sopha" and several mahogany "hair-bottomed" chairs covered in the same material as the curtains. There would also be a "lolling" chair, a pair of mahogany card tables with a pair of gold-framed looking glasses above, and often a pianoforte, tall and "banjo" clocks, pictures, mantel objects of pottery or porcelain, lamps, decanters, wineglasses, japanned ware, candlesticks, candelabra, and other silverware. The popular tea equipage included trays, urns, caddies, spoons, and a "tea sett of china."

Chinese export porcelain, including the so-called "Lowestoft," was often made to order. The water front of Canton was lined with wharves flying the American and

Chinese Export Porcelain creampot with the Arms of the Cincinnati

European flags. Here the merchants traded and shipped home crates of these popular dishes. Four famous tea sets inscribed with the *Arms of the Cincinnati* were brought to America for George Washington, Henry Jackson, General Benjamin Lincoln, and Captain Samuel Shaw. One may be seen at the Concord Antiquarian Society, and other pieces of exportware belonging to prominent Boston families are in the Museum of Fine Arts and local collections. The *Order of the Cincinnati*, named for Lucius Quinctius Cincinnatus, the famous Roman soldier who left his plow to serve the state, was founded in 1783 by Washington's officers to help each other when in need and "To Perpetuate friendships formed during the War." George Washington was the president until his

Blue Staffordshire printed ware with a view of an English Country House

death. This distinguished hereditary society is still very active today. The cream jugs of these and other Chinese export porcelain tea sets also show the classic influence of the period in their shape, a Roman helmet inverted.

In addition to this oriental porcelain there was also some French porcelain, English Staffordshire and other pottery.

The blue Staffordshire printed ware was very popular for dinner and tea sets. Many pieces had views of English country houses or American buildings. Those with the State

House, the Bulfinch Building at the Massachusetts General Hospital, and other early Federal Boston buildings are still very much sought after. Many interesting buildings now gone may be seen on these dishes.

The household inventory of the Joseph Cutler Estate is a valuable record. The list of furnishings of each room in his home on Orange Street, now Washington Street, and other inventories show us how Bostonians lived in this early Federal period.

McLean Hospital, Sommerville, Massachusetts, 1811

Inventory of the Estate of Joseph Cutler late of Boston in the County of Suffolk Merchant deceased, taken Decr 18th 1806

Wearing Apparell &c

Item	Amount
10 Coats & Surtouts – 12 Waistcoats 15 Pr Pantaloons & Small Cloaths 17 Pair Stockings 3 Hats – 3 Pair Boots – 4 Pair shoes 2 flannel Waists 6 Shirts – 5 Neck Cloths	75.. 00
1 Gold Watch chain	17.. 00

Front Parlour Chamber

Item	Amount
Bed, Bedstead 2 Blankets, 2 Sheets Counterpain & Curtains	50.. 00
1 Bed Quilt 1.50 Bureau $11 Writing Desk $3.50	16.. 00
Trunk 1.50 Brass Andirons Shovel & Tongs $13	14.. 50
6 Silver Table spoons 13.50 – 1/2 Doz Teaspoons $11..25	24.. 75
Mustard spoon 50 – Sugar Tongs 1.50	2.. 00
Tea Tray & part sett China &c $5 Small Tray & 14 Fruit plates $1	6.. 00
Plated Castor & Cruits $4 5 Tumblers $1	5.. 00
Large Bible Small Do & 14 other Books	10.. 00
Carpet 13.33 Hearth Rug $2	15.. 33
13 Sheets 16..25 – 7 Coarser Do – 5..25 2 Doz Pillow Cases $7	28.. 50
6 Table Cloths 10.50 – 4 Breakfast Do $2 – 5 Common Table Cloths $6	18.. 50
18 Towels 1.80 Looking Glass $12 – 2 old Blankets $2	15.. 80

Middle Chamber

Item	Amount
Bed, Bedstead 2 Sheets 1 Blanket bed quilt Counterpane & Curtains	25.. 00
Lolling Chair $4 Bureau $4 Night Chair $5 6 Chairs $4	17.. 00
2 Trunks $2 Iron Shovel & Tongs 75 Looking Glass 3.50 Inkstand 25	6.. 50
49 Books $16..33 Curtain at entry Window 1.50	17.. 83

North Bed Chamber

First page of the Inventory of the Estate of Joseph Cutler, Boston, 1806

INVENTORY

of the Estate of Joseph Cutler late of Boston in the County of Suffolk Merchant deceased, taken Decr. 18th 1806

WEARING APPARELL

10 Coats & Surtous – 12 Waistcoats 15 pr Pantaloons & Small Cloths 17 Pair Stockings 3 Hats – 3 Pair Boots – 4 Pair shoes 2 flannel vests 6 Shirts – 5 Neck cloths	75.00
1 Gold Watch chain	17.00

FRONT PARLOUR CHAMBER

Bed, Bedstead, 2 Blankets, 2 Sheets Counterpain & Curtains	50.00
1 Bed Quilt 1.50 Bureau $11 Writing Desk $3.50	16.00
Trunk 1.50 Brass Andirons Shovel & Tongs $13	14.50
6 Silver Table spoons 13.50 – ½ Doz. Teaspoons $11.25	24.75
Mustard spoon 50 – Sugar Tongs 1.50	2.00
Tea Tray & part Sett China $5 Small Tray & 14 Fruit plates $1	6.00
Plate Castor & Cruits $4 5 Tumblers $1	5.00
Large Bible Small Do. & 14 other Books	10.00
Carpet 13.33 Hearth Rug $2	15.33
13 Sheets 16.25 – 7 Coarser Do. 5.25 2 Doz. Pillow Cases $7	28.50
6 Table Cloths 10.50 – 4 Breakfast Do. $2 – 5 Coarser Tablecloths $6	18.50
18 Towels 1.80 Looking Glass $12 – 2 old Blankets $2	15.80

MIDDLE CHAMBER

Bed, Bedstead, 2 Sheets, 1 Blanket, bed quilt Counterpain & Curtains	25.00
Lolling Chair $4 Bureau $4 Night Chair $5 – 6 Chairs $4	17.00
2 Trunks $2 Iron Shovel & Tongs. 75 Looking Glass 3.50 Inkstand .25	6.50
49 Books $16.33 Curtain at entry Window 1.50	17.83

NORTH BED CHAMBER

Bed, Bedstead 2 Sheets 1 Blanket 2 Quilts Curtains	$ 25.00

KITCHEN CHAMBER

Bed Bedstead 2 Bolsters & 3 Pillows	12.50
1 Bedstead 1.50 Trunk Containing 7 pieces Bed covering $12	13.50
Chest & 2 Baskets	2.00

EAST LITTLE CHAMBER

2 Beds 2 Sheets Blanket & Coverlid	30.00
	$447.71

FRONT WEST ROOM

1 Sopha & covering $25 Pr. Card·Tables & Coverings $18	43.00
10 Chairs $15 – Pr. Looking Glasses $40	55.00
Pictures of Washington and Adams 2.50 – 20 Yds. old Carpet $10	12.50
2 Tea Trays & Coffee-Sett Crockery $4 – 2 Green Table Cloths $8	12.00
Table sett China $20 Tray with Ivory Sett Knives & Forks $14	34.00
Coffee & Tea Sett Liverpool Ware $4.50 Glassware in Closett $5	9.50
Castor & Cruits $12 – 2 Pair plated Candlesticks $3	15.00
Teapot Sugar bowl and Creampot plated $15 Pr Brass Lamps .75	15.75

FRONT ENTRY

Dining Table $6 – Stair Carpet $2 – 2 pair fire Buckets & 2 Bags $8	16.00

MIDDLE ROOM

Clock $35 Dining Table $5 – 1 Do. $5 Breakfast Do. $3.50	48.50
Looking Glass $12 Lolling chair $3 – 2 Arm Chairs 2.50	17.50
½ Doz. chairs $5 Rocking do. $1 – 2 Childrens Do $1 – Cradle $4	11.00
Carpet $5 Hearth rug $2 Hand Irons shovel & Tongs $13	20.00
Back Gammon Board 1.50 Liquor case with Bottles $6	7.50
Bellows & Brush $1 Waiter with 2 pr. decanters pr Salts, Tumblers & Wines $5	6.00
In Closett, plates, dishes, Tureens, 4 pitchers, 2 Canisters & Tray	6.00

STORE ROOM

4 demijones 2.80 – s Stone jugs 1.50 – 3 baskets & a Tub 1.50	5.80
Mahogany Stand 2.50 – 1 Maple do. – .75 Tray wt. Knives & forks 2.50	5.75
Box small tools	2.00

CELLAR

2 Casks potatoes $3 – Ullage Wine 12.50 – 2 pipes sour cyder $12	27.50
Ullage Keg Molasses 3.20 – 3½ Doz American porter $7	10.20

KITCHEN

6 polished dish covers $6 – 6 Do. Tin 1.50 Tea & Coffee pots 1.50	9.00
Tin Tea Kettle 2.50 Cheese Box .75 Bell mettled Kettle $3 Mortar $1	7.25
Set Crockery ware Pudding dishes plates etc $2 – 6 Iron Flats 1.75	3.75
4 Bread pans 1.33 Hand Irons Shovel & Tongs 2.50	3.83
Copper Tea Kettle 2.50 2 Tables 1.50 folding Board .33	4.33
Warming pan $2 Looking Glass .62 Brush & Broom .50	3.12
3 Candlesticks Lamp Tinder Box shoe brushes Snuffers & Bellows	1.37
	$860.86

Brought forward	$860.86

SINK ROOM

Brass Kettle $7 2 Iron pots, 3 dish Kettles Bakepan Iron Tea Kettle small pot & Skiller $6.50	13.50
Coffee Mill 1.50 Grid Iron & Toaster – $1	2.50
Tin Roaster $2, frying Pan, tub, Pole & Clothe Line $1	3.00
Tin ware	2.50
2 Pair Brass Candlesticks in Keeping Room	3.33

WOOD HOUSE

Cupboard with shelves 1.50 25½ Doz. bottles @ .58	16.29
Tubs & Casks $6 – Wood $10 – 2 Cloathe horses $1.50	17.50

WOOD HOUSE CHAMBER

Stone pots and Charlestown ware $4 Lanthorn $2	6.00
Coffee Roaster, plate warmer, water pot, Coffee mill & Bread Trough	2.50
3 Cheese Boxes .75, Empty Cask, tubs, Boxes Baskets, etc	3.50
Ullage Barrel Meal	.50

BARN & YARD

1 Cow $18 – 2 tierces Vinegar 8.50 Wheelbarrow .50	27.00
Bark $6 – part Barrel Soap .75 shovel, Butle & Hoe $1	7.75
Glas Case	2.50
	$969.23
6 Chamber Chairs @ 10/6	10.50
Benja. Goddard, David W. Child Sam. Dorr	$979.73

Inventory of the Stock in trade of Joseph Cutler and Asa Whitney under the Firm of Cutler and Whitney, one half of which belonging to the Estate of the said Joseph Cutler of Boston County of Suffolk. March 1 deceased, taken Decr. 19th 1806

13..2.0 Cod Fish	@ 4.00	54.00
6½ Barrels Brown Sugar 12..1.2	@ 10.00	122.68
5 do. Havana Sugar 6..2.15	@ 14.00	92.87
12½ Casks ordinary Tobacco 1603 lbs	@ .08	128.24
14 do. Good do. 2222 lbs	@ .15	333.30
637 lbs Sole Leather	@ .20½	130.58
4.3.14 Copperas	@ 4.00	19.50
3.3.21 Indin Allum	@ 5.50	21.65
596 lbs Coffee	@ .30	178.80
1 Barrel 2 half Barrels & 12 Kegs Ginger 636 lbs.	@ .12	76.08

2 Bags Pepper – 197 lbs	@	.18	35.44
2 Barrels Garlicky Flour	@	6.00	12.00
154 lbs White Rope	@	.10	15.40
8½ Chests Hyson Tea – 552 lbs	@	1.11	612.72
7½ do. H.Skin do. 476 "	@	.60	285.60
5 do. Souch do. 421 "	@	.70	294.70
Ullag Gunpowder Tea 18 "	@	1.20	21.60
do. Young Hyson do. 79 "	@	.95	75.05
221 lbs Bengal Indigo	@	2.00	442.00
111 lbs. do. do. (ordinary)	@	1.25	138.75
0.3.7 – Rice	@	4.25	3.46
37 Bales Cassia 391 lbs	@	.36	140.76
2 Boxes, 5 half Boxes and Ulage No. 1 Chocolate 206 lbs	@	.32	65.92
3 Boxes @ .25 & 5 half ditto for Ditto	@	.20	1.75
25 Gunny Bags	@	.09	2.25
20 lbs Salt Peter	@	.20	4.00
24 Yards Tow Cloth	@	.20	4.80
11 lbs Spun Yarn	@	.08	.88
434 lbs Snuff	@	.25	108.50
18½ lbs Bottles	@	.22	3.96
107¼ lbs do.	@	.12	12.84
30 lbs Loaf sugar	@	.21	6.30
39 Baskets	@	.28	10.92
18 Demijons	@	.90	16.20
			$3473.52

1½ Chest Bohia Tea 575 lbs		@	.40	230.00
11.1.21 Logwood		@	3.10	35.45
5 Hhs. 3 Barrels & Ullage Molasses 616 gr.		@	.37	227.92
1 Ullage Cask Raisins 30 lbs		@	.08	2.40
26 Rheam Writing Paper		@	2.88	74.88
1 Pipe Containing 44 Gals. Ginn		@	.95	41.80
3 Pipes 100 Proof Burdox Brandy	316 Gs	@	.75	237.00
1 Do. 200 do do do	52 Gs	@	.80	41.60
4 Do 4th proof Barcelona Brandy	405 gs	@	.83	336.15
4 Hhs St. Croix Rum	414 gs	@	.85	351.90
1 do Jamaica do	107 gs	@	.88	94.16
22 do Tobago do	2267 gs	@	.72	1632.24
2 Box Brimstone 3.1.0		@	4.00	13.00
3 Pipes white wine	303 gs	@	.85	257.55
2 do Cape do	212 gs	@	.84	169.50
1 Do Sherry do	68 gs	@	1.00	68.00

4 Qr Casks sherry wine	132 gall	@ 1.18	115.76
21 Gallons Cargo Nidonia Wine		@ .95	19.95
1 Pipe Marcella Madeira do	84 gall	@ 1.00	84.00
Ullage Cognac Brandy	52 gall	@ 1.15	59.80
4 Casks Red Wine	227 Gall	@ .60	136.20
1 do do (damaged)	55 gall	@ .20	11.00
2 Barrels No. 3 Mackrell		@ 7.00	14.00
3½ Doz. Porter Bottles		@ .58	2.03
12 half Barrels		@ .66	7.92
12 Kegs		@ .20	2.40
A Quantity of Sea coal		@ 11.00	11.00
85 Bags fine Salt		@ 3.25	276.25
Ullage Keg Essence Spru		@ 6.00	6.00
20 lbs dipt Candles		@ .12½	2.70
15 Bushels Beans		@ 1.50	22.50
8 Galls. Colouring		@ .90	7.20
8 Cheese Casks		@ .42	3.36
28 Sugar Barrels		@ .30	8.40
5 Molasses Hhds		@ .90	4.50
2 Empty Pipes		@ .90	1.80
2 Rum hhds		@ 3.00	6.00
1 Medicine Chest		@ 4.00	4.00
			$8137.96

1 Large Seale Beam & Rigging		@ 23.00	23.00
2 Small do do do		@ 2.50	2.50
1 Copp. hand Pump Measures & Tin funnells			15.00
26 half Cwt. Weights		@ 1.75	45.00
2 28 lb. Weights		@ 1.00	2.00
3 14 lb. do		@ .62	1.86
3 7 do		@ .37	1.11
6 11 do		@ .28	1.68
4 2 do		@ .14	.56
1 Sett Brass Weights		@ .75	.75
2 Water Pails and Wooden Funnell		@ 2.00	2.00
1 Chest Store Tools		@ 8.00	8.00
1 Book Chest		@ 4.00	4.00
1 Writing Desk		@ 9.00	9.00
1 Map United States		@ 8.00	8.00
4 Painted Wine Casks		@ 11.00	11.00
1 Guacigeing Rod			3.00
5 Wine Casks		@ 1.00	5.00
312 lbs & 687 lbs Cheese	999 lbs	@ .10	99.90

151 lbs Lump Butter		@ .18	27.18
1 Barrel Old Beef		@ 8.00	8.00
5 Kegs poor Butter	232 lbs	@ .15	34.80
10 Barrels Mess Beef		@ 11.75	117.50
57 do No. 1 do		@ 9.75	555.75
35 do No. 2 do		@ 7.75	271.25
9 do No. 3 do		@ 5.75	51.75
3 Kegs second Sort Butter Inspection included 133½ lbs @ .18 Inspection @ .07			24.24
6 Old Sugar Hhds and Tierce			2.33
Old Boxes .75 3 Old Cheese $1.00			1.75
			$9476.37
More Indigo 26		@ 1.25	32.50

Benj. Goddard, David W. Child Sam. Dorr

Sundries at Store at South End VIZ:		
6 Casks Vinegar 223 Gallons	@ .12	26.76
6 Casks for do.	@ 1.37	8.22
Old Cask in Cask Yard	@ 10.00	10.00
2 Iron Shovels	@ .50	1.00
1 Half Bushel, Peck & half-peck measure	@ .33	.33
1 Beef Block $1.00 1 Pork Block $7.00		8.00
1 Grindstone $3		3.00
5 old Barrels & Tubs	@ 1.20	1.20
1 Pork Hook	@ .25	.25
16 half Barrels and Old Cask	@ .25	4.00
4 Bushels Oates & Pease	@ .50	2.00
4½ do Rye (damaged)	@ .62	2.79
1 Bedstead Bed & Bedding	@ 16.00	16.00
1 Fire Settle	@ 1.50	1.50
Skillet Dish Kettle & Old Iron	@ 1.50	1.50
Old Casks Kettles Hammers etc	@ 3.00	3.00
		$9598.42

Suffolk Ss. At a Probate Court held at Boston on Monday the Nineteenth day of January Anno Domini 1807 — Phabe Cutler Administratrix on the Estate of Joseph Cutler late of Boston in said County Merchant, Deceased, presented this Inventory and made Oath it contained all the estate of said deceased, that had come to his hands and knowledge that if she should hereafter be possessed of any thing further she will render and account for it into the Probate Office. Thomas Dawes Judge of Probate

Examined John Heard

Bostonians' Country Houses

Wealthy Boston families not only lived in stately town houses but also had country seats in the English manner. Several of these exist in what is now greater Boston, and some may be visited.

Most of these estates had extensive grounds and large mansion houses, reflecting the contemporary seats that dotted the English countryside. Bulfinch possessed books from abroad showing these great houses: Among them were *Original Designs in Architecture* by William W. Thomas, published in London in 1795 with elevations and plans for a bow-front house. Most of the great American country houses of the early Federal period had a bowed section framing a lovely oval room inside, although many were called circular or bow parlors in those days.

Pleasant Hill, the country home of Joseph Barrell of Summer Street, was built in 1792 in Charlestown (now Somerville) and overlooked the Charles River. Approached by a driveway bordered with English elm trees, it had gardens at the rear extending down to the water and a private dock from which his boats transported his family to Boston. This fine brick mansion with a bow front had the usual oval room, classic interior finish, and a magnificent divided staircase. Later it was enlarged, with wings added by Bulfinch, and became the McLean Hospital for the Insane. The original house remained unchanged until 1896 when it was demolished and the hospital moved to the present location in Waverly.

Mrs. James Swan of Chestnut Street, Boston, built her country home in Dorchester in 1796. This swell-front wooden house, set high on a grass terrace, had famous gardens accented with white-painted statues of fauns and nymphs sent from France. There was a family tomb on the grounds, a few minutes' walk from the house, enclosed by a tall lilac hedge. The beautiful circular parlor in the center of the mansion, known as the Marie Antoinette Room, had three mirror windows and superb French furniture. Here in 1825 she entertained at a reception for her old friend, the Marquis de Lafayette.

Nearby Mr. Perez Morton's country house was also the scene of many brilliant gatherings in the early Federal period. This distinguished mansion with a pedimented and pilastered façade had a semicircular entrance porch with a Wyatt window above, a recessed fanlighted entrance door, a rich cornice, and a roof rail. There was a fine classic stable beyond the turf terrace and curved carriageway. Inside was an oval room, but this house had no bow front.

These country seats had a great variety of architectural detail, although the interior plans were often similar. * Mr. Stephen Higginson's large house, built in 1798 in Brookline on the old Sherburne Road (later part of the Worcester Turnpike), reflected different British ideas. The staircase was in a separate room off the entrance hall or entry, a feature unique in this country, and the dining-room ceiling was decorated with the raised plaster ornament of wheat and grape motifs so characteristic in England at the time. Although altered, this house still has the marble mantels, Wyatt windows, and a bow-ended parlor.

Harrison Gray Otis had his country seat, named ** Oakley, in Watertown. The wooden farmhouse which he

Interior of Shirley Place, Roxbury, now known as the Shirley-Eustis House, showing the Federal staircase in Governor Eustis' country house

purchased was built in 1715 and was pleasantly situated on a hill affording an unbroken view of Cambridge and Boston. In 1808 he rebuilt this house and added the popular architectural features of his day. Among these were the bow front, framing an oval room, and two staircases — a rectangular back stairs leading to the top of the house and a graceful winding front stairway ascending to the second floor. This circular flight of steps is one of the few extant with double railings of mahogany terminating in scrolls. Here Otis lived a rural life in the hot weather and entertained gay house parties until 1825. Much of his house remains incorporated in the clubhouse of a golf club which still bears the old name of Oakley.

The large square country seat built earlier by the well-known colonial Governor Shirley on Roxbury Hill was also partially remodeled at this time. A black-and-white checked stone floor like those in the great English country houses was laid in the entrance hall and a graceful curved staircase replaced the simpler colonial one. Here in this historic house both Washington and Lafayette were entertained. Now known as the * Shirley-Eustis house, this important governor's mansion still stands and it is hoped that it will soon be restored to its former dignity.

Two of the largest and finest country seats of Boston gentlemen are in Waltham and both are open to the public for a small fee. *Gore Place* is maintained by the Gore Place Society and *The Vale* by the Society for the Preservation of New England Antiquities.

** *Gore Place* was built in 1804 by Christopher Gore, three years before he was elected governor, to replace his earlier wooden country home which had burned during his absence in England. This long, low, two-story brick mansion of twenty-two rooms, so like Heaton Park near Manchester, England, has a bow front framing two oval rooms, twenty by thirty feet, one above the other. Unusual in this country is the billiard room on the ground floor, similar to the one in the handsome British residence. Other features are two fine fanlighted entrance doors opening from a stone terrace, a magnificent "flying" spiral staircase, marble floors, beautiful mantelpieces, and a dignified two-story music room. An 18th-century wooden ** stable now houses a collection of carriages. The Gore Place Society hopes to restore the extensive grounds to the original plan, with gardens, an orchard, shade trees, a grape arbor, pastures with a ha-ha wall, deer park, and a Mile Walk, to form the proper setting for this great American country house.

Gore Place, Waltham,
the country house of Governor Christopher Gore

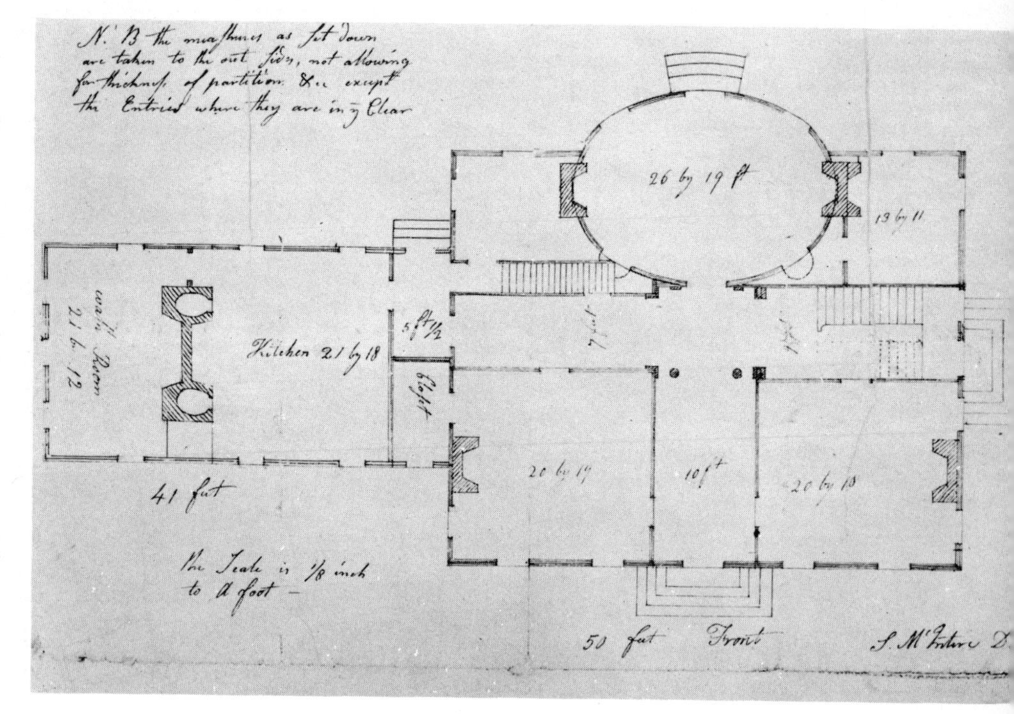

Plan of The Vale, Waltham, the country house of Theodore Lyman, by Samuel Mc Intire

The ha-ha, so customary in English grounds, is a ditch about four feet in depth which drops off sharply at the end of the mowed lawn supported by a retaining wall on the high side. This separates the lawn from the pastures beyond and prevents the cattle from approaching the house. The term ha-ha came from the amusement caused when people unknowingly stepped over the edge and into the ditch!

Theodore Lyman, whose Boston house was in Bowdoin Square, built his fine country seat, ** *The Vale*, in 1793, from plans by Samuel McIntire (1757–1811). These are now in the Essex Institute, Salem. The large wooden mansion house still retains the oval room known as the "Bow

The Vale, now the property of The Society for the Preservation of New England Antiquities

Parlour" with the original window seats and other pieces of furniture, and the distinguished ballroom with a colonnaded end, formerly the library. Photographs hanging inside show the exterior of the house as it was when it was built, of white clapboards with pilasters on the upper façade and a balustrade on the roof. A fine McIntire stable also survives.

The original estate was of one hundred and fifty acres, but within a few years Mr. Lyman purchased three hundred additional acres. He brought over a well-known English gardener, William Bell, who planned the grounds in the manner of Humphry Repton (1752–1818,) the great British landscape architect of the late 18th century. Several seasons were required to grade and lay out the ** gardens which today are considered the finest of their type existing in America. The park, a mile in length, was enriched by English limes, elms, and oaks along with other foreign shade trees. There were broad lawns, a deer park, a pond with swans, and a brook crossed by two stone arched bridges. There was also a box hedge four feet high and a peach wall where the fruit trees were trained in the French espalier manner. This old wall of brick, about eleven feet high and five hundred feet long, follows the curve of the hill behind the mansion and leads to the greenhouses.

These ** greenhouses, built in 1800 and 1804, are among the oldest and most unique in the country. They had a quaint system of heating. One was warmed by a long, flat, horizontal flue running the length of the house and connecting with a small wood-burning fireplace. All this remains and was in use as late as 1931. The other was heated by small wood fires in the arches of brick at the base of the brick north wall. This heating of the wall gave out the necessary warmth. Here were raised pineapples, bananas, and other tropical fruit, ornamental plants and flowers. Very old camellias still blossom profusely and an ancient grapevine continues to bear delicious fruit. These interesting old "glass-houses," the grounds, and mansion house are now open to the public in the summertime.

The Lyman family has always been interested in horticulture. In 1792 Mr. Lyman founded the Massachusetts Society for the Promotion of Agriculture and later, his son, Theodore Lyman, Jr., when mayor of Boston in 1835, had a fine alley of trees planted on the Common from Park to West streets, forming a mall. These shaded the fashionable "promenade" and are still standing.

The Town Becomes a City

In 1822 Boston was incorporated as a city. At about this time quarries were opened in Braintree, now Quincy. The granite from these and other quarries transformed Boston from a red-brick town to a city predominantly of gray stone. New public buildings and some residences reflected this change. Even streets were paved with granite blocks. Previously the small amount of stone used, principally for the trim of brick buildings, was taken from the surface of the ground. In the early 19th century stone was brought from Chelmsford by way of the Middlesex Canal. After the quarries were opened large quantities of great granite blocks were also hauled over rails from Quincy to Neponset by a team of sixty-five yoke of oxen and twelve horses. Then they were shipped across the harbor to Boston. This granite railway was built by Gridley Bryant, the engineer, father of Gridley J. F. Bryant, the well-known Victorian architect. It is said to have been the first railroad in the country and the forerunner of the great system of passenger and freight railroads of the Victorian era.

The Granite Railroad, West Quincy, 1826

The Greek Revival in Boston

The granite period brought in a new kind of architecture, that of the Greek Revival, still classic, but on a larger scale, plainer, and with more solid dignity. It was transitional to the monumental, richly carved style seen in Boston later in the 19th century. Well into the Victorian period this massive granite-classic simplicity continued to replace the delicate wooden cornices and other classic ornaments of the early Federal era.

New architects designed many of these buildings, among them Alexander Parris (1780–1852), a native of Hebron, Maine, who came to Boston after serving in the War of 1812, and Isaiah Rogers (1800–1869), who later became the outstanding hotel architect of the country. Benjamin was also working in the new style.

Science, shipping, and industry were making great strides and provided the fortunes that financed this new upsurge in building, which began after the recovery from the War of 1812. The American Academy of Arts and Sciences had been established in 1796. The Harvard Medical School, founded in Cambridge in 1782, had moved to Boston in 1810. Both of these distinguished societies are still contributing enormously to the welfare of their fellow Americans.

The First Boston Hospital, Bulfinch building at the Massachusetts

Hospitals

Boston's start as a great medical center dates also from the end of this early Federal period. In 1818 Bulfinch designed the first building of the ** Massachusetts General Hospital on the shore of the Charles River in the West End. It was his last commission in Boston, and his friend Alexander Parris took over the supervision of the building when Bulfinch moved to Washington. This handsome hospital, one hundred and fifty feet long, is of Chelmsford granite. Reflecting the quiet dignity of the Greek-Revival style, it is raised on a high basement and terminates in the new-style, shallow, saucer-like dome. The stately façade has a pedimented portico of massive smooth Ionic columns above the basement story, a lunette window in the pediment, and four

General Hospital, 1818, showing the rope walk building at the far right

chimneys surmounting the top corners of this impressive center block. The high portico is approached by a pair of graceful granite staircases with iron railings, and is now flanked by wings added in 1846.

The interior, beautiful in its simplicity, still retains the fine arches, the groined elliptical ceilings, and the granite staircases with their smooth round Roman column-style balusters of iron and graceful, curved wooden handrails. The floors are of solid granite blocks, about two by four and a half feet, except in the basement where they are of red tiles seven and a half inches square.

Here in 1846, in the operating room under the great dome, Dr. John C. Warren administered ether for the first time in a surgical operation. This beautiful building is in use today, another example of a fine old architectural landmark still fulfilling its original purpose.

Detail of the Bulfinch building at the Massachusetts General Hospital

Dr. Oliver Smith founded the first Dispensary in Boston in 1796. Incorporated in 1801, it was the third in the country and is functioning today on the same street. Here, at the corner of Bennet and Ash streets, the original building was a three-story Federal mansion of brick with stone lintels and a beautiful fanlighted doorway. The Dispensary was then supported by private charity and the staff of physicians gave their services. In recognition of his services Dr. Smith was presented by the city with a fine set of Chinese export porcelain. Some pieces of this china, now in the Museum of Fine Arts, show French influence in the delicate

Chinese Export Porcelain presented by the City of Boston to Dr. Oliver Smith, founder of The Boston Dispensary

18th-century design inscribed with his initials in script. This type of cypher was a very popular monogram on silver as well as china.

The Massachusetts Eye and Ear Infirmary was also founded at this time by Dr. Edward Reynolds and Dr. John Jefferies. Incorporated in 1826, this important hospital is still serving the public.

Chinese Export Porcelain, ten gallon punch bowl

St. Paul's Cathedral by Alexander Parris

Churches

** St. Paul's Cathedral (Episcopal) initiated the new style in churches in Boston. Built on Tremont Street in 1820, it now stands tucked away between larger and later buildings. Near the Park Street church, it offers an opportunity to view at one glance the striking contrast between the two classic styles, early Federal and Greek Revival. This temple structure of granite with a pedimented portico of Virginia sandstone was designed by Alexander Parris. There was to have been sculpture in the pediment, but this was not executed due to lack of funds. The great smooth columns were made in sections or drums as were those on the ancient Greek temples. The beautiful Ionic capitals were carved by Solomon Willard.

An earlier church of Chelmsford granite had been built in 1814 by Bulfinch. It overlooked the harbor on the site where Summer and Bedford streets converge. This New South Church, known as the Octagon Church because of its shape, also had a portico and may be seen not only in old prints but on many blue Staffordshire printed ware plates.

The New South or Octagon Church, by Bulfinch

Portrait of Josiah Quincy
by Gilbert Stuart

Granite Markets and Warehouses

One of the splendid new granite buildings was the ** Quincy Market, built beside the beautiful old brick Faneuil Hall Market in 1824 by Alexander Parris. These buildings offer a comparison of the best in the two Federal-classic styles. Like Faneuil Hall, the Quincy Market is still serving its original purpose.

It is five hundred and fifty-five feet long, two stories high, and has a noble portico at each end. The central saucer-like dome is sheathed with copper. The four stately smooth columns on the porticoes, great shafts of granite twenty feet nine inches high, are among the finest monolithic columns

East View of Faneuil Hall, the Quincy Market and warehouse drawn by J. Andrews

in Boston. These one-piece columns were replacing the earlier drum or sectional type used on St. Paul's Cathedral and were considered a great feat of engineering in that day.

The market was named for Josiah Quincy, Jr., the mayor of Boston at the time and a member of the famous family that gave our country two presidents. He opened up this market district in the old colonial North End without imposing extra taxes or debts on the city. From 1824 to 1826 the flats were filled in, worthless old buildings along the water front were demolished, and six new streets were laid out, paved with granite blocks and lined with great granite warehouses.

Many of these fine solid buildings, unexcelled anywhere, remain today and may be seen from the elevated highway.

Faneuil Hall and the Quincy Market

Granite warehouses

The Custom House by Ammi B. Young showing the original dome

Other Granite Structures

** The Custom House, one of Boston's finest Greek-Revival buildings, was built on the water front facing the docks. This impressive granite building, designed by Ammi B. Young (1800–1874) and erected on three thousand piles, is now well inland. Built from 1837–1847 in the temple style with a portico, it terminated in a shallow saucer-like dome with a skylight and was surrounded by thirty-two fluted monolithic columns weighing forty-two tons each.

Later, when more space was required for offices, a tall tower was added, thus saving most of this outstanding building from destruction.

Detail of the Custom House showing the monolithic columns

Custom House tower,
a later addition

Bunker Hill Monument

The old granite Court House of 1810 was designed by Bulfinch with the octagon center surmounted by a cupola and with his characteristic arched window recesses on the façade. It stood on School Street on the site of the present City Hall and when it was unfortunately demolished in 1862 some of the granite was used for the new building.

The great granite obelisk, the ** Bunker Hill Monument, which pierces the skyline so effectively, was built in Charlestown to commemorate the famous battle fought there in the Revolutionary War. Solomon Willard won the competition for the monument with his Egyptian design, although some had favored a Roman column, as both these styles were popular at this time. In 1825, on the fiftieth anniversary of the battle, the aging General Lafayette came to Boston to lay the cornerstone. It was an important celebration, with an oration by Daniel Webster and much entertaining.

The famous obelisk, thirty feet square and two hundred and twenty-one feet high, set a fashion for this style of monument. Willard was partial to granite and later gave up carving and designing to be in the quarry business. Two of his smaller granite obelisks are the tombstone erected in memory of Franklin's parents in the old Granary Burying Ground in 1827 and the well-known monument of Carlisle granite set up in 1825 at the Concord Bridge.

The first "modern hotel" in Boston was the famous Tremont House at the corner of Beacon and Tremont streets, beside the old Granary Burying Ground. It was built in 1828–29 from designs by Isaiah Rogers. This wonderful old hotel of white Quincy granite was a large rectangular block with a symmetrical façade accented by a stately Doric portico of four columns. A central cupola on the original design was never built and the usual hostel stable was also eliminated.

The Tremont House was the first to provide many new conveniences. There were single and double sleeping rooms instead of the large rooms with several beds found in the colonial inns. Each room had a lock on the door, a wash-basin and pitcher set, a cake of soap, and a lamp. Rain-water cisterns supplied the new-style washrooms in the basement and there were eight of the recently invented "water closets" on the first floor to serve the occupants of the one hundred and seventy bedrooms. These new facilities which were replacing the colonial outhouses were also installed, with much trepidation, in the new State House.

The Tremont House, by Isaiah Rogers, 1829

The Tremont House had ten elegantly furnished public rooms lighted by gas. The "grand lobby" had columned walls and a dome ceiling of richly colored stained glass. The main dining room overlooking Beacon Street accommodated two hundred people. One chose food from a menu, instead of taking the only meal served, as had been the custom in the earlier inns. The bill of fare was extensive. Here Thackeray first tasted American oysters and in 1842 Charles Dickens stayed at this well-known hotel and wrote a description of it. This famous old building was demolished in 1894.

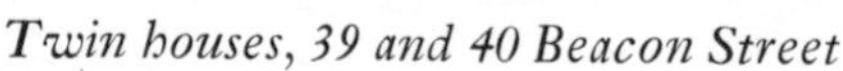

Twin houses, 39 and 40 Beacon Street

Doorway at 40 Beacon Street

Greek-Revival Residences

Although some notable granite mansions were built in Boston, of which a few remain, domestic architecture in the Greek-Revival period continued to be of brick with stone ornaments. The style changed, however. Bow fronts and heavier classic iron balconies became increasingly popular. Delicately fluted columns gave way to large, smooth Roman types, and fanlights over the entrance doors were replaced by transoms filled with rectangular panes like the windows. Houses in this late classic style had a simplicity and a solidity not found in the earlier Federal homes. The last houses to be built on Beacon Hill, with the exception of a few Victorian homes added later, were in this style.

Block of granite town houses, on Beacon Street west of River Street, attributed to Asher Benjamin

In 1835 Cotton Hill to the east was leveled to become Pemberton Square. The celebrated mansion of Gardiner Greene set in terraced gardens overlooking Boston harbor was demolished. Mrs. Greene, a daughter of John Singleton Copley, the well-known colonial portrait painter whose land was bought by the Mount Vernon Proprietors, moved to Beacon Street. She had a desire to save one of the rare trees from her former home, a Chinese ginkgo. With much difficulty this tree was moved to the Common opposite her new home, at the corner of Joy Street. Today, more than one hundred and twenty-five years later, it still stands, frail but bearing fruit which is much sought after by the Chinese who come early in the morning to gather it.

Nearby are the charming twin houses at 39 and 40 Beacon Street, built in 1818, now the ** Woman's City Club. This handsome pair of brick dwelling houses with

The Sears Mansion, 42 Beacon Street, by Alexander Parris at the right and beside it

bow fronts and recessed entrance doors, flanked by large smooth Roman columns, had an upper story added in 1888. The interiors, although changed, retain two magnificent circular staircases sweeping gracefully to the top of the house. They are lighted by an oval roof window or skylight. One of these stairways also has two wall niches, and both have the plain, smooth round balusters characteristic of this period. There is also some rich Greek-Revival carving on the trim of the second-floor parlors.

Just down the Hill, at what is today * 42 Beacon Street, Alexander Parris built a splendid Greek-Revival granite house for Colonel David Sears, now the Somerset Club. This was the site of the old Copley dwelling house and is now marked by a * plaque. Built in 1819, the Sears mansion is a

on the left the third Harrison Gray Otis House showing the bow-end at the side

stately bow-front house of which the entrance and one bowed section are original, while the second bow was added later on the site of the garden. The beautifully carved panels on the façade are the work of Solomon Willard.

A fine block of six uniform * granite town houses of smaller size was built in 1828 on the water front of the Charles River before the Back Bay was filled in. It is attributed to Asher Benjamin. The houses now face the Public Garden on Beacon Street, west from River Street. Designed as three double houses, each one had a beautiful dormer with an arched window and corner pilasters of Greek-key detail with a pediment above. The River Street end of the block is of brick with stone lintels, also of Greek-key detail, over the windows.

Louisburg Square

Lovely old ** Louisburg Square, pronounced "Loois-burg," running between Pinckney and Mount Vernon streets, was the last part of Beacon Hill to develop. Legend has it that the first white settler of Boston, William Blaxton or Blackstone, whose farm covered most of the area in the 17th century, obtained his water from a spring here and springs occasionally break through this part of the Hill to-day. The square is thought by some to have been named for the colonial battle at Louisburg, Nova Scotia, fought in 1748, when the French were driven out and the Atlantic seaboard was secured for the English. Many Bostonians took part in this battle.

One hears stories of the lavender glass windowpanes, seen in the Square and elsewhere on the Hill. These are not rare or always old, although some do date from 1818–1824. The lavender color resulted from the sun's rays on imperfect glass.

Like an old London square framed by dwelling houses, Louisburg Square remains residential in the heart of a great city and is outwardly much the same as it was in the 1840's. In 1826 S. P. Fuller drew a plan for the Square or open space and "the streets paralled therewith," including the park to be "surrounded with an open fence or railing." Lots were laid out overlooking this park, but it was not until the building boom of the 1830's that the first lot on the upper Pinckney Street corner was sold in 1834. Most of the houses

Louisburg Square in winter

were built in the late 1830's or 1840's. In 1844 the Square was enlarged and took its present bow-ended rectangular form. The tree-shaded park with its grass, shrubs, and two statues — Columbus at one end and Aristides at the other — flanked by cobblestone carriageways, is privately owned and maintained by the abutters except on the Mount Vernon Street side.

Through the years many interesting and well-known people have lived in these stately Greek-Revival houses. William Dean Howells resided at number 16, Louisa May Alcott at number 10, and Jenny Lind, the Swedish singer, visited and was married at number 20, to mention just a few. In recent years the custom of lighting the windows with candles on Christmas Eve has become associated with Beacon

Louisburg Square in summer

Hill and especially with Louisburg Square. On this night the Hill is perhaps at its best, with the old inside shutters open and the candles softly illuminating the beautiful Federal interior architecture and furniture, while carol singers mingle with the crowds outside. Some prefer it in summer when it is quiet, or in the spring when the trees are budding in soft lacy greens against the old red of the bricks, while others prefer it in the winter etched with snow or with the shadows of twilight; but to all it is charming.

Time has been kind to ** Beacon Hill. The cobblestones are still there in the Square in spite of the coming of

Louisburg Square at sunset

the automobile. The beautiful old Greek-Revival houses with their pedimented doorways have the same dignity as ever, although many now have apartments within instead of single-family homes. Bells toll as they always have in the Charles Street Meetinghouse nearby and from St. Margaret's Episcopal Convent on the Pinckney Street corner. In a world of turmoil the rosy glow at sunset on the fine old Federal houses and old brick sidewalks reflects peace, security, and beauty. It will always remain so, for, under the protection of a recent law, much of Beacon Hill, including the Square, has been made an "Historic District."

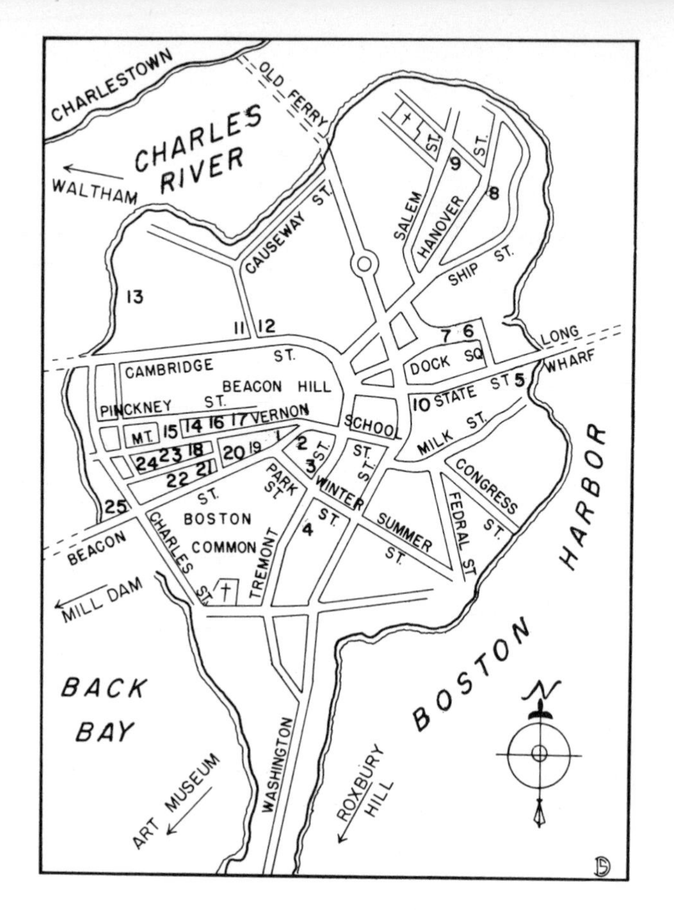

HISTORIC SITES OF FEDERAL BOSTON

1. Massachusetts State House
2. The Amory-Ticknor House
3. The Park Street Church
4. St. Paul's Cathedral
5. The Custom House
6. The Quincy Market
7. Faneuil Hall
8. St. Stephen's Church
9. The "Old North Church"
10. The Old State House
11. The Harrison Gray Otis House, HEADQUARTERS OF THE SOCIETY FOR THE PRESERVATION OF NEW ENGLAND ANTIQUITIES
12. The West Church
13. The Bulfinch Building at the Massachusetts General Hospital
14. 74 Pinckney Street
15. Louisburg Square
16. 87 Mount Vernon Street
17. 85 Mount Vernon Street
18. 13, 15, 17 Chestnut Street
19. 39, 40 Beacon Street
20. 42 Beacon Street
21. 45 Beacon Street
22. 54, 55 Beacon Street
23. Acorn Street
24. 9 West Cedar Street
25. The Charles Street Meeting House

A SUGGESTED TOUR OF FEDERAL BOSTON

for the hurried, intelligent traveler

Begin by taking a taxi or the subway to Park Street Station to the *Massachusetts State House* on Beacon Street on the top of Beacon Hill.

After visiting the interior walk down Park Street past the *Ticknor House* and the *Park Street Church* to *St. Paul's Cathedral.*

Taxi or subway from Park Street Station to Washington Street Station. Change and go to the State Street Station. Walk two blocks down State Street to the *Custom House.* Walk (a short distance) over Commercial Street and left on South Market Street to the *Quincy Market* and *Faneuil Hall.* Walk under the elevated highway to Hanover Street to *St. Stephen's Church* and the *Old North Church* and back to *Faneuil Hall.*

Taxi or subway from the *Old State House* to Bowdoin Station via the East Boston Tunnel. Walk two blocks to the *Harrison Gray Otis House* and the *West Church* at the corner of Cambridge and Lynde streets.

Take a taxi, a bus, or walk down Cambridge Street to Anderson Street — five blocks (Massachusetts General Hospital on right). Walk or taxi four blocks up Anderson Street to Pinckney Street (now the steepest part of the hill). Look back down Anderson Street to the *Bulfinch Building,* the original Massachusetts General Hospital. Walk down Pinckney Street one half block to number 74 and 74½. Enjoy one of the loveliest views down Beacon Hill across the Charles River to Massachusetts Institute of Technology. Walk down the Hill one half block to Louisburg Square and through the Square to Mount Vernon Street. Then up the Hill one block past two *Bulfinch Houses* numbers 87 and 85, the latter the second *Harrison Gray Otis House* and the one-story former carriage houses to Walnut Street. Down Walnut Street, two blocks toward the Common to Beacon Street, looking down Chestnut Street on the right to the *Bulfinch Houses* numbers 13, 15, and 17.

On Beacon Street pass *numbers 39 and 40* Twin houses (now the Women's City Club), *number 42* the granite *Sears mansion* (now the Somerset Club), *number 45*, the third *Harrison Gray Otis mansion* with its stable in the rear (now the American Meteorological Society), and the twin houses *numbers 54 and 55* (now the headquarters of the Colonial Dames of Massachusetts.)

Turn right on Charles Street and then first right on Chestnut Street and first left on West Cedar Street. Look up the old cobblestoned *Acorn Street* on the right. Pass number 9, *Asher Benjamin's* house, and pause at the corner of Mount Vernon to look down at the *Charles Street Meetinghouse*.

Taxi from Charles Street or take bus at Storrow Drive to Copley Station and the subway via a Huntington Avenue car to the *Museum of Fine Arts* to see the Gilbert Stuart paintings, Federal furniture, and silver, including the Paul Revere bowl and pitcher.

INDEX

Index